HOW TO DISCOVER YOUR FAMILY HISTORY

using free resources!

Anthony E. Trice

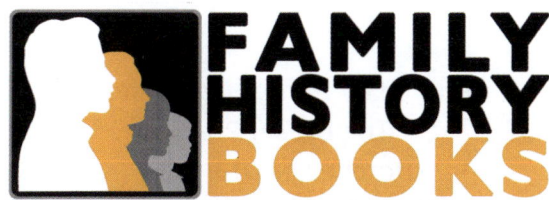

FAMILY HISTORY BOOKS

www.familyhistorybooksonline.com

Published by
Family History Books
the publishing imprint of the
Family History Federation
a registered charity number 1038721
P.O. Box 62
Sheringham, Norfolk
NR26 9AR

ISBN: 978 1 916599-00-0

First published 2023

Printed by Henry Ling Limited
The Dorset Press
Dorchester DT1 1HD

Contents

Acknowledgments

I wish to acknowledge the contributions made by the learners from my local U3A and library; they helped me develop the beginners' course in family history which forms the basis of this book.

My sincere thanks are due to Dorothy, Sue, Marian, Rosemary and Pam from my local U3A and Viv and Blanche from the local library. My thanks also go to Suzie who proofread my drafts and provided some very useful advice for the book cover design.

My thanks to the late John Morton of the Hampshire Genealogical Society for the use of his family history exercises.

I am also indebted to my mother-in-law who stimulated my interest in researching her family tree. But the most important thanks are to my wife, Ann, for her love, support and encouragement throughout our life together.

Introduction

It is difficult to pinpoint the exact date or period when family history and genealogy became popular, but there is no doubt that in this busy buzzing twenty-first century, more and more people are embracing this absorbing hobby every day. Years ago researching one's family was a long drawn-out process which involved going through dusty old books in cavernous cold buildings or traipsing round graveyards, pencil and paper in hand. Well, forget all that now! With fast digital communications, a wealth of informative websites plus popular television programmes like *Who Do You Think You Are* and *Long Lost Family,* family history has climbed the ladder and become one of the world's favourite hobbies – no matter what your age!

There are many good books on genealogy covering a wide variety of detailed issues, but few seem to cater specifically for the needs of beginners in respect of what can be found where on the Internet – and these days that's where everyone turns to for help and guidance. Having taught a family history course at my local library for some years, it became clear to me that people wanted to know what they could find on the Internet for free – and more specifically, how to do it! Thus, the seeds for this book were sown!

The aim of this book is to provide a step-by-step guide to accessing genealogy websites - and to do so as cheaply as possible. Family history can be an expensive hobby but much of the basic information you need to start your research can be done using free resources. Starting with information you already know about your family, I will show you how to work backwards to find your ancestors' records.

The book concentrates mainly on English and Welsh records. How to research your Scottish ancestors is well covered on the Scotland's People website but it is a pay-to-view service. You can search their indexes free of charge; you only need to use pay-per-view to inspect and download digital images of the records you find.

A word of warning! When writing this book in September 2022, I used images from the various websites; but do remember that websites change their design and layout quite frequently. However, the research principles remain the same, so if a website you find is a little different from my illustrations, you should still be able to find the records of your ancestors.

Researching one's family history is an absorbing hobby and it can indeed become somewhat addictive! You will find sections at the back of the book giving lists of further reading and useful website links and other information on various sources and historical background.

I hope this book will prove to be a useful introduction to the first stages of researching your family history; it will cost you nothing but your time. But once you are hooked, the sky's the limit! So, why not give it a go!

Chapter 1

Summary

This chapter provides information on the history of the records you will use and how to conduct your own research. It concludes with a couple of exercises to start you on the journey towards discovering your ancestors.

History

Long before the Internet and computers, the only way to research your family tree was to visit a local register office, a county record office or Somerset House in London to look for post-1837 birth, marriage, death and census records. The county record offices hold parish records of baptisms, marriages and burials. The general record office occupied Somerset House from 1836 and in 1970 the records were transferred to St Catherine's House. Eventually St Catherine's House was closed and the records could then be searched at the Family Records Centre [FRC] in Clerkenwell London from 1997.

On 21 June 2006, it was announced that The National Archives' staff and residual services at the FRC would be relocating to The National Archives at Kew by the end of 2008. During October 2007 the index volumes of births, marriages and deaths were gradually removed from public access to a closed archive in Christchurch, Dorset. The FRC closed on 15 March 2008.

Before the Internet it was a long process to find records because there were no commercial or free indexes to help you find the information. The birth, marriage and death registers were large books with one book for each quarter of a year. These registers were in effect an index to the event certificate. You needed to know roughly when your relative was born, got married or had died and then use the appropriate register to search the alphabetical list to find the reference which you would use to order the certificate. Marriages were more difficult as you needed to know the maiden name of the bride to find a match to the reference number of the groom.

To access census records you had to have some idea as to where your ancestors lived, and then search through a microfilm to find the relevant image. It was a laborious process!

Years ago I would go to London for the day and would count myself lucky if I found a record or two! Nowadays it is easy, maybe too easy, to trace a few generations using the Internet in a couple of hours of research. As a result, we now expect to find references to our ancestors but wonder why we cannot do so on all occasions.

What is Family History?

There are three main areas of research.

- **Genealogical research**
This involves collecting names and dates of birth, marriage and death of your ancestors and building a family tree.

- **Biographical research**
This puts *flesh on the bones* by finding out about their actual lives, where they lived and what they did for a living.

- **Historical research**
This will put your ancestors in the context of the political, economic and social history of their times.

How do I start?

This hobby will generate a lot of paper and one of the skills you need is the ability to manage a lot of information. To begin with you will need a notebook to record your findings. Each ancestor you find should have a page or two in your notebook. Here you will write down the information you find about your ancestor's birth, marriage and names of their children. Each child will also warrant a section of your notebook.

Eventually you may consider creating a family tree on a computer by inputting this data.

The first step is to create a plan so that you know what you want to achieve.

What is my research plan?

There are several ways to research your ancestral tree. Before you start researching, you need to decide on your plan. You could choose one of the following:

- The most common plan is to track down all the direct ancestors of your mother and father.

- You could decide to trace the male line in your family. This will include father, grandfather, great-grandfather and so on. You will also discover the names of their wives, brothers and sisters.

- The same approach could be taken for the female line but as a woman changes her surname on marriage, this can be more difficult.

- Another approach is to find all the descendants of an early ancestor. This, however, is the most difficult approach.

- A final method is to track down all those with the same surname, regardless of relationship to the researcher. This is known as a One-Name Study.

This book will demonstrate how to research using the first and most common option - finding out about your direct ancestors. Start from information you know such as your father's birth date and then work backwards. Later you may want to choose an historical ancestor and trace all their descendants towards the present day. These will not be your direct ancestors but will include aunts, uncles and cousins.

Once you have decided on your plan you need to know how the subscription and free websites work. Some of the websites use unpaid volunteers to transcribe the record information into a searchable database or index.

Most of the post-1837 birth, marriage and death registers have been transcribed and will be found on the FreeBMD website. The volunteers were given copies of the pages from the original register books from which they transcribed the names, districts and references into a searchable database. In addition, the General Register Office (GRO) now offers a free searchable index for birth and death registers making it easy for you if you need to order the appropriate certificate.

The commercial websites like Ancestry, Findmypast and others also have their own searchable databases of the life events. In fact, Ancestry has the FreeBMD index for the period 1837 to 1915 and has its own index from 1916 to 2007 [2005 for marriages].

Census records run from 1841 in ten-year intervals to 1921 and are available on the subscription websites. The Latter-Day Saints Church, or LDS church, has a website of transcriptions of census records; but unlike the subscription websites, it does not have images of the records. The LDS was the first organisation to transcribe the 1881 census; this and other census records are available as transcriptions of households or families. The LDS records will be found on the Family Search website.

The 1921 census was released in 2022. At the moment this can be found on the Findmypast website and you will have to pay for a copy of the transcription and for a copy of the image of the record. You can view the 1922 census for free at The National Archives at Kew.

Another free website for census records is FreeCEN but the number of transcriptions they show is dependent on how many volunteers they have!

Pre-1837 parish registers of baptisms, marriages and burials can be found at local county record offices along with a multitude of other useful local information. The LDS website also has some parish records but once again coverage is dependent on volunteers. The same can be said for the free website FreeREG which also relies on volunteers and their own interests.

Some of the county record offices have provided copies of their parish records including images to the subscription websites who have created an index to these records. But coverage is limited.

I have a plan so what do I do now?

Having decided on your plan to find out about your direct ancestors, the first thing to do is write down everything you know about your parents. This will be their birth dates and date of marriage. Do you have certificates which will be proof of these facts? Can you repeat this for your four grandparents and for your eight great-grandparents? Don't worry if you cannot do so - I will guide you through the steps to finding your ancestors.

The aim is to find and confirm all the life events such as birth and marriage dates.

How do I reference the records I find?

You must remember to record all the information you find including the website and date on which you found the data. I will provide ideas on how to keep track of your research.

Surnames
I record the surnames in capital letters keeping the woman's name as her maiden name, for example, **Janet SMITH.**

Births, marriages and deaths
The **SOURCE** is recorded as either a **GRO REFERENCE** or as a **CERTIFICATE** if you have one.
The **SOURCE** is referenced as shown in these examples:

Certificates
> **1893 Birth certificate John READER**
> **1913 Marriage certificate John READER and Janet SMITH**

GRO References
Year GRO Event Index District Quarter Volume Page and name of ancestor

> **1913 GRO Marriage Index Plymouth Jun 5b 2 John READER and Janet SMITH**
> **1973 GRO Death Index Plymouth Dec 5b 67 John READER**

Parish records of baptisms, marriages and burials.
I use the method as shown in these examples.

> **1767 Parish register of baptism John READER**
> **1788 Parish register of marriage of John READER and Janet SMITH**

Census
Details of the **CENSUS** data are recorded as an **EVENT** like births, marriages and deaths.

Year Census HO or RG No, Piece number, Folio number, Page number, Name of head of household

> **1901 Census RG 13 1086 Folio 78 Page 11 John READER**

The 1911 census has a different reference numbering system as shown below. You will find the reference on Findmypast on the transcription page and on the Family Search website.

> **1911 Census RG 14 13033 RD 278 SD 2 ED 3 Schedule 52 John READER**

On 29 September 1939, a few weeks after war had been declared, a **National Register** was taken to enable the Government to issue identity cards, ration books and identify all those who could be called up for military service. The 1939 reference will also be found on the transcription page as **RG101/0668G/005/20 Letter Code: BACF.**

The 1939 National Register index is on the Findmypast and Ancestry websites.

The 1921 census reference is similar to the 1911 one and if you buy the transcription you will find the full reference as given in this example.

1921 Census RG 15 10727 RD 278 SD 2 ED 30 Schedule 19 John Reader

Images
If an image of a census page is held, then the file name for your image is the same as the source name.

Exercise One

Complete a box-shaped diagram like the example below for as many of your ancestors for whom you have information.

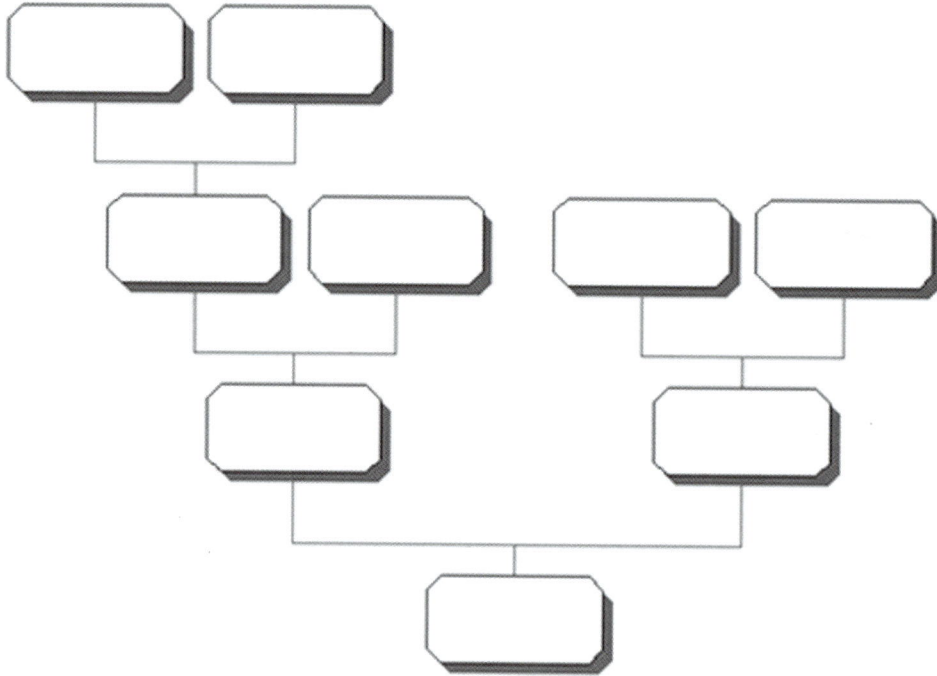

Exercise Two

Not all information comes in a concise format. Some of your evidence may be letters or conversations with relatives. For example, you may find a family bible, photos, postcards, letters etc.

If you are going to interview a relative it is recommended you record it. Listen to your relatives carefully and check spellings. Watch for nicknames, shortened names or the use of a second name in preference to a first name. Check relationships with your relative. Who married whom and which children did they have? In which county and parish did they live?

Not everyone will remember all the details accurately so be ready to confirm any information you are given. The exercise on the next page will help you to interpret any information you discover from a talk with a relative. The answers will be found at the back of the book.

1. Draw a family tree from the information in the conversation shown on the next page.

2. Add as much detail as possible.

3. Identify what is missing and what you would need to do to verify the information you have.

Notes taken by me, John Henry Christopher Fleet, in conversation with my father John Fleet in June 1970.

1	JF	So, you want to know something about your ancestors?
2	Me	Yes – your grandson is doing a project at school on family history. I have provided him with my birth and marriage details and what I know about you, Dad. I know I was named after you and my second name came from my grandfather. Is that correct?
3	JF	How is Jonathan getting on at school?
4	Me	He is doing well especially in mathematics. So, my name?
5	JF	Oh yes. Yes, you are named after my father, Henry Fleet. He was born in Devonport, but he died during the second year of the Great War when I was two. I have visited his grave in Belgium with your mother and grandmother a year after our marriage. Six years before the next World War. It only seems like yesterday.
6	Me	You were married in London, weren't you?
7	JF	I met Caroline when I started my first job in London. She was my landlady's daughter. Now her family is much more interesting than mine. Do you want to know about her family too?
8	Me	No, just yours. Jon has been told to concentrate on his grandfather's side of the family. So where does my third name come from?
9	JF	My grandfather Christopher. He died a year after your mother and I got married. Your uncle was named after him as well. He was born two years before me. Your aunty Mary two years after that and she was named after my grandmother.
10	Me	What can you tell me about grandma? I know she remained a widow.
11	JF	I am not sure how my mum and dad met. She doesn't talk much about those times. She married dad in her late teens. I do know that they had been married five years before he was killed. Her family helped after that. It could not have been easy bringing up three children on her own.
12	Me	What was grandma's name? I only ever heard her called Pip.
13	JF	That was her father's pet name for her. She was Elizabeth Farnham Odiham.
14	Me	That sounds rather grand. Farnham is a town in Surrey, isn't it?
15	JF	And it was her mother's maiden name. In fact here is a snapshot of my parent's wedding. Mum has scribbled on the back "my parents, Albert and Hannah to my right next to my grandparents George and Edith."
16	Me	What I would like to do is to draw out the family tree and check it with you before I go. A diagram will help me explain it to Jon when I get home next week.
17	JF	I'll put the kettle on. Are you sure you don't want your mother's family tree as well? It has some scandal and mystery! Her mother was Theodora – what a name! Her father had a bit of a reputation – married twice – first wife died or so it was said.
18	Me	No, I'll just stick to your family.

Chapter 2

Summary

This chapter shows you how to find the basic evidence you need to build your family tree. It provides a step-by-step guide to using the FreeBMD website in order to obtain information about post-1837 births, marriages and deaths. There is an exercise to help you use the website before you start looking for your ancestors.

Collecting the evidence

Family history research is like detective work and you need to gather the evidence which includes:

- Birth certificates or GRO reference links
- Marriage certificates or GRO reference link
- Death certificates or GRO reference links
- Census records
- Other historical records such as parish records.

Having one piece of evidence is not enough proof. For example, someone reports having seen me in my local high street on my mobile phone. It is their word against mine! However, my mobile phone log could place me in the high street at the right time. Now there are two pieces of evidence! It is the same for genealogical research where we need to have at least two sources of information for an event such as a birth or marriage.

However, not all evidence is clear cut. For example, if you have an original birth certificate then that is strong evidence and can be treated as a **primary** source. If you only have the GRO reference then this is **secondary** evidence. What one of your relatives tells you about your family members is at best **questionable**. What you need to try to do is to convert your sources to primary if you can. But obtaining copy certificates can be expensive so this book will show you how to support your secondary sources with other information.

Some argue that for a source to be considered primary it must be an original document in your possession. This is not always possible as you are never going to possess an original census document. The closest you can get is an image of a census page from a commercial website. Personally, I would label these as primary.

Genealogical Proof Standard

The Genealogical Proof Standard is a process used by genealogists to demonstrate what the minimums are that genealogists must do for their work to be credible.
(Information from FamilySearch website
www.familysearch.org/en/wiki/The_Genealogical_Proof_Standard_(National_Institute).)

This genealogical standard lays out five essential steps for accurate research.

1. **Have you looked at all the records?**
   Births
   Baptisms (from parish registers)
   Marriages
   Banns or licence records (from parish registers)
   Deaths
   Burials (from parish registers)
   Census records
   Other records

2. **Complete accurate source citations**
   The citation tells you and others where you found the information. Was the evidence from a website, an original certificate or a parish record? You need to record the source. For example:

   GRO index - Year, quarter, district, volume and page numbers
   Census - Year, HO or RG number and piece, folio and page numbers

3. A **source** is a birth certificate, a baptism record or census image. A birth certificate will have the name of the child and at least the name of the mother. The **source** can be used as evidence of the names of all child and parent or parents. The link to the **source** is known as a **citation**. The **source** will be cited in individual records of the child and the parents.

4. **Analysis and correlation of collected evidence**
   Look carefully at the evidence. Do the ages match? Is the place consistent with all the sources? Do the family members match? Annotate your evidence as original, secondary or questionable.

5. **Resolution of any conflicting evidence**
   If conflict is found, then search again and gather further evidence. Review the new evidence.

6. **Can you write a soundly reasoned and coherent conclusion?**
   Finally, can you write a sentence or two demonstrating how you reached your conclusion.

Conventions

I always record the surnames with capital letters as these are easier to find in a list or report. The women retain their **maiden** names in your family tree. However, when referencing them in a source after marriage, use the married name in capitals. This would apply when the married woman is recorded in a census record or for her death or burial record.

Another convention is to use a pencil to record the information as it is easy to rub out and amend your data. In addition, county record offices like pencils!

Organising your information

As you develop your family tree, you will probably have lots of notes in a notebook or on individual pieces of paper. Before you go too far, you need think about how you are going to organise your information.

I have already mentioned using a notebook. Some people use a card index for everyone they research with cross references to their family, spouse and children. Some of you might be using computer-based software to record all your information.

There is a good guide on the Family Search website WiKi and you can find it by typing this link into your web browser.

www.familysearch.org/wiki/en/Organize_Your_Genealogy

What can I do if I cannot find an ancestor?

Here are some reasons why you cannot find your ancestor, and some suggestions as to what more you can do to improve your chances of finding an ancestor.

- The record may have been mis-transcribed. Remember...the volunteer transcribers are reading handwriting that is not always easy to interpret. Try alternative spellings or use the phonetic search option if available.

- Remember...if you are looking for a female ancestor, after marriage her surname will have changed to her married surname for a census and death or burial records.

- Normally you would be looking for the woman using her maiden name for a marriage, **but**, if she remarries, she will be using her previous married name.

- If you cannot find your ancestor in one website database, then try another.

- As you will discover, not all life events or census records were recorded, preserved or transcribed.

- Sometimes our ancestors changed their names for all sorts of reasons. They may use a second forename as they do not like their first forename.

- There is always the possibility that you will fail to find the record of an ancestor. These are called *brick walls* and the most obvious is the birth of an illegitimate child.

Examples from my own research

I could not find my maternal grandmother in the 1911 census where she would be living with her parents. I discovered that her father had entered all the family members with just their initials - not with their first names. I found her by searching for D HOBBS.

I expected to find my parents in the 1939 register but I knew this same grandmother was living with them at the time. I found her name in the record and the image showed my parents living at the same address. However, the transcriber had interpreted the T of TRICE as a capital I. So they were indexed under IRICE!

The brother of one of my great-great-grandfathers disappeared in one of the census years. It was years later that someone contacted me to explain what had happened. He was in the Royal Navy and for some reason he had jumped ship and arrived in Australia where he changed his name, married and had a family! On his death bed he announced to the family his real name. So no longer was he missing in my family tree.

So...do not give up! You should find your elusive ancestor unless the record as been destroyed or they changed their name for some reason.

Further help

Helen Osborn has written an excellent book on research methods. If you want to find out more the book is entitled *Genealogy – Essential Research Methods* and is published by Robert Hale. [ISBN 978-0-7090-9197-4].

Let's get researching!

I am going to use my own family to demonstrate how to carry out your research. We will start with a free website FreeBMD.

FreeBMD is an ongoing project, the aim of which is to transcribe the civil registration index of births, marriages and deaths for England and Wales, and to provide free Internet access to the transcribed records. FreeBMD is constituted as a charitable trust, and supported by hard-working volunteers; the primary objective of the site is to transcribe all the index entries from the commencement of civil registration in September 1837 up to 1983.

George and Louisa Trice in the 1940s.

If you have Scottish ancestors you will need to use the website ScotlandsPeople. The indexes are free of charge but you need to pay for an image.

When searching FreeBMD it is important not to enter too much information. You need to be reticent about specifying middle names; sometimes these were only added when a child was baptised, so they won't appear on the birth certificate. In later years only middle initials are shown in the index.

If there are too many results to display, you will be asked to modify your search criteria by adding some other facts or reducing the range of years searched.

A good principle to follow is to enter as little as possible into your search criteria. Remember... *enter LESS information to get MORE results*. If you get too many hits enter a little more data.

What did I actually know when I started investigating my family tree? My father was the youngest of eight children and his father was George TRICE. Dad told me that my grandfather was in his 70s when he died in the 1940s. So his birth date is going to be around 1870. My dad was born in Devon so I could assume that his father was born in the same county. I knew my grandmother was a Louisa CREBER.

A new version FreeBMD is due in 2023

As this book went to press there was the possibility that the website for FreeBMD would be revised to match the style used for FreeCEN and FreeREG both of which we will meet later in the book.

If and when this change happens, there is a distinct possibility that there will be a link on the new website to the old FreeBMD website that I have detailed in the next couple of chapters. On the new website, the same principles for your search will apply and you will see the boxes to enter names and to select counties and districts.

How do you use the FreeBMD website?

> **Note:**
>
> Throughout the book I have used the word <u>screen</u> to refer to the <u>website image</u> you will see on your computer and page to refer to the page of this book. For clarity I have in some cases only shown you part of the website image.

1. Using your Internet web browser, enter **www.freebmd.org.uk** and press the **Enter** key on your keyboard. You will get the welcome screen similar to that shown below.

Welcome to FreeBMD.

FreeBMD is an ongoing project, the aim of which is to transcribe the Civil Registration index of births, marriages and deaths for England and Wales, and to provide free Internet access to the transcribed records. It is a part of the Free UK Genealogy family, which also includes FreeCEN (Census data) and FreeREG (Parish Registers). To search the records that have so far been transcribed by FreeBMD click on the **Search** button below.

The recording of births, marriages and deaths was started in 1837 and is one of the most significant resources for genealogical research. The transcribing of the records is carried out by teams of dedicated volunteers and contains index information for the period 1837-1997, **BUT WE HAVE NOT YET TRANSCRIBED THE WHOLE PERIOD.** A breakdown by event and year can be viewed here.

FreeBMD is exactly that - FREE. **We do not make any charge whatsoever for use of the site and we never ask for credit card details to do a search.** FreeBMD is a registered charity and our objective is to provide free online access to the GRO Index. However, FreeBMD costs money to run and if you would like to make a donation, by PayPal or other methods, please see here.

[Search] [View Images] [Information] [Join FreeBMD] [Transcribers' Page]

The FreeBMD Database was last updated on Sat 4 Jun 2022 and currently contains 288,530,711 distinct records (380,101,174 total records).
On Thu 6 Oct 2022 FreeBMD users did 109,557 searches. (More information)

2. Click on **Search** and the Search screen below will appear. For a full explanation of the search fields click on the word **Help**.

3. In the **Type** options in the top left-hand corner tick the **Birth** box.
4. Enter surname and the first forename in the labelled boxes. As I was looking for my grandfather I entered TRICE in the **Surname** box and George in the **First name(s)** box. FreeBMD will find all those with second names.
5. Enter **Date range** to Mar 1870 to Dec 1879.
6. Select Devon from the **Counties** table.
7. Only select from the **Districts** table if you are sure that it is the correct one.
8. If you have entered these details, you should then have a screen that looks like this.

9. Click the red **Find** button to see results from the search criteria.
10. If you have tried this yourself you will not get any results. Therefore we must have entered some data that is invalid.
11. This is the display you should see.

Sorry, we found no matches.

Search for	Type:	Births	Surname:	Trice	First name(s):	George
	Start date:	Mar 1870	End date:	Dec 1879	County:	Devon

12. I assumed that George TRICE was born in Devon. So we need to remove that selection.
13. Click the red **Revise Query** button to amend the search query. You will see this screen.

14. Below the **Counties** table click **select all**. Then click the red **Find** button.
15. If you have no luck the name might not be transcribed correctly. For example TRICE might have been reported or incorrectly transcribed as TRYCE.
16. If you click the **Phonetic search surnames** box in the **Options** section you will get a list of names that *sound like* the surname you have entered.
17. The next screen shows you the list of TRICEs I found when I selected all counties and did **not** use the phonetic search option.

Surname	First name(s)	District	Vol	Page		
Births Sep 1870 (>99%)						
Trice	George William	E. Ashford	2a	665	Info	✍
Births Mar 1871 (>99%)						
TRICE	George	Brighton	2b	260	Info	✍
TRICE	George Frederick	Thanet	2a	814	Info	✍
Births Jun 1871 (>99%)						
Trice	George Thomas	Portsea	2b	453	Info	✍
Births Mar 1872 (>99%)						
TRICE	George William	Sheppey	2a	810	Info	✍
Births Mar 1874 (>99%)						
Trice	George W V	Elham	2a	923	Info	✍
Births Dec 1876 (>99%)						
TRICE	George	Steyning	2b	278	Info	✍

18. I do not know if my grandfather had a middle name so he could be any one of the seven people shown.
19. Don't despair if this happens to you. I will show you in a later chapter how to identify which one is my grandfather.
20. Let us look at an entry and explain what is shown and what the icons will show.

Surname	First name(s)	District	Vol	Page		
Births Sep 1870 (>99%)						
Trice	George William	E. Ashford	2a	665	Info	✍

21. If this was my grandfather the source reference for his birth would be **1870 GRO Birth Index Sep E. Ashford Volume 2a Page 665 George William TRICE [accessed on FreeBMD on 12th December 2022].**
22. The district [East Ashford] in which the event was registered is shown in blue.
23. Clicking on the blue **District** name will open another tab in your browser giving you information about the district.

FreeBMD

District Information

Surname	Given Name	District	Volume	Page
		Births Sep 1870		
Trice	George William	E. Ashford	2a	665

The district **E. Ashford** is an alternative name for **East Ashford** and it is in the county of **Kent**; information about it can be found here

There is more information on Districts, and how FreeBMD handles them, in the Registration District Information page.

Close Window

24. This shows you the county or counties which the registration district covers.

25. You will need to close the new tab to return to the screen of entries by clicking on the **Close Window** button.

26. If you click the word **here** at the end of the sentence under the birth reference, it will provide a list of parishes within the district in a separate window in your internet browser as shown on the next page.

27. You should see two tabs in your web browser. One has a title **FreeBMD Search** and the second has the title **East Ashford Registration District**. You can see these at the top of the image on the next page.

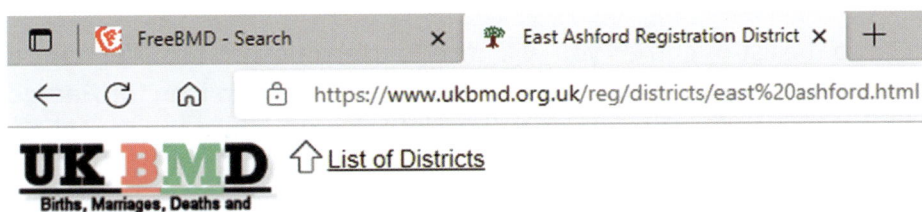

FreeBMD - Search   ×   East Ashford Registration District   ×   +

https://www.ukbmd.org.uk/reg/districts/east%20ashford.html

UK BMD
Births, Marriages, Deaths and
Censuses on the Internet

⬆ List of Districts

EAST ASHFORD REGISTRATION DISTRICT

- *Registration County* : Kent.
- *Created* : 1.7.1837 (originally "Ashford East").
- *Abolished* : 1.4.1941 (to become part of **Ashford** and **Folkestone** registration dist
- *Sub-districts* : Aldington, Brabourne, Wye.
- *GRO volumes* : V (1837-51), 2a (1852-1941).

Table 1: List of

Civil Parish	County	From	To	
Aldington	Kent	1837	1941	See Table 2, notes (a), (b), (f), (h)and (i)
Ashford	Kent	1934	1941	That part which until 1.4.1934 formed pa
Bilsington	Kent	1837	1941	See Table 2, notes (h) and (i).
Bircholt	Kent	1837	1934	Abolished 1.4.1934 to become part of th

28. If you get to this screen you will need to close the tab in your web browser labelled **East Ashford Registration District** to return to the list of entries. To do this click the little cross in that browser tab.

29. You will be returned to the list of names. Clicking on the blue **Page** number will give you a list of all births in that quarter in the district. This is useful as if twins were born both names would appear on the page.

30. This is the screen you will see listing all the births in East Ashford in the 1870 September quarter.

| Search for | Type: Births | Start date: Sep 1870 | End dat |
| | Volume: 2a | Page: 665 | |

Whilst FreeBMD makes every effort to ensure accurate transcription, e an entry has the symbol ↩ next to it you can view the scan of the GRO

If you are SURE that our transcription(s) below differs from the GRO i

Surname	First name(s)	District	Vol	Page

Births Sep 1870 (>99%)

Surname	First name(s)	District	Vol	Page		
DEAL	Albert	E. Ashford	2a	665	Info	↩
HUBBARD	Lydia	E. Ashford	2a	665	Info	↩
Jarvis	Jane Mary	E. Ashford	2a	665	Info	↩
Law	Harry	E.Ashford	2a	665	Info	↩
Mepsted	David	E. Ashford	2a	665	Info	↩
Mileham	Florence Maria	E. Ashford	2a	665	Info	↩
Rogers	Ureita	E. Ashford	2a	665	Info	↩
ROGERS	Uretta	E. Ashford	2a	665	Info	↩
Trice	George William	E. Ashford	2a	665	Info	↩
VAUGHAN	Barbara Jane	E. Ashford	2a	665	Info	↩
WILES	Ada Jane	E. Ashford	2a	665	Info	↩

31. To return to the list of entries you will have to use your web browser back button.
32. In the main list of entries for 1870 to 1879 click the red **Info** icon for George William TRICE to open a screen showing you who transcribed the entry into the FreeBMD database.

FreeBMD

Entry Information

This entry was created from the following transcriptions:

Surname	Given Name	District	Volume	Page	Transcribers
		Births Sep 1870			
Trice	George William	E. Ashford	2a	665	picl
TRICE	George William	E. Ashford	2a	665	Cornwall

33. When you have finished, scroll down and click the **Close Window** button at the bottom left-hand side of the screen to return to the list of names.
34. Clicking the spectacles icon will take you to a screen where you can find an image of the original index book page.

View the original

FreeBMD will _never_ ask for credit card details to view the orginal

Help with this facility

Use of this facility is subject to your acceptance of the **Terms and Conditions of Use**

You can view the original scan that was used to transcribe this entry. The following is a list of scan files that contain the entry.

LDS-211-000-0951645/1870b3-460.tif
ANC-05/1870B3-T-0460.jpg

Select which file you wish to view (by clicking on it), select the format using the buttons on the right and then click on the **View the original** icon on the left. Unless the entry is absolutely clear in the scan you view, we strongly suggest you view all the scans as some may have a clearer rendition of this entry.

If none of the scans above contain the entry you may be able to find the scan yourself by clicking here. If one of the scans does not contain the entry you can leave feedback by clicking here.

Display scan in following format:

○ gif
○ jpeg
○ tiff
○ pdf
◉ original

Which format to choose?

If FreeBMD has been of help in your search you may wish to consider making a donation.

Citations

You can use one of the following citation references to refer to this entry:
URL https://www.freebmd.org.uk/cgi/information.pl?cite=uP6gHIPOPGC%2BOyExbFxVBg&scan=1
Wikipedia {{Cite web|url=https://www.freebmd.org.uk/cgi/information.pl?cite=uP6gHIPOPGC%2BOyExbFxVBg&scan=1|title=Index entry|accessdate=8 October 2022|work=FreeBMD|publisher=ONS}}

Postem

A Postem is a note left by someone about this record - the content of the postem is determined by the person who left it. FreeBMD can offer no assurance about the postem and will not enter into correspondence about it. You can leave a Postem by clicking on **Add a postem**. Further information about Postems is available here.

Close Window

35. This is where you choose how to display the image and advice on which format to choose. The format will depend on what your computer can display.

36. When you have finished, scroll down and click the **Close Window** button at the bottom left-hand side of the screen to return to the list of names.

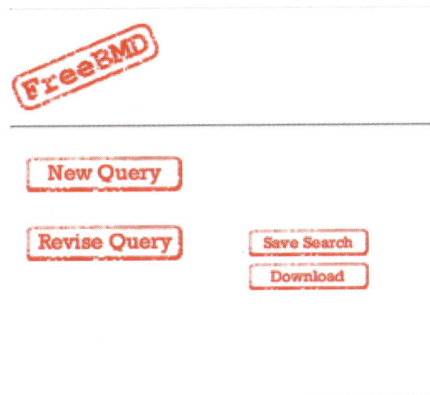

37. You now carry out another search by clicking the **New Query** button on the left-hand side of the screen. If you have finished searching, close your browser.

The next step is to record what you have found - or not found. You can do so in a number of ways. You could have a notebook, index card or a form of your own design. In this case I would record that George TRICE was not born in Devon but he could have been born in one of the registration districts that appeared in the FreeBMD screen.

Now you need to plan what you are going to do next. Some people record this in a _To Do List_ or a _Research Log_. Usually, my next step would be to look at the census closest to the birth year for the individual. But in this case I am not sure which George TRICE is my grandfather. Therefore I will look for the marriage of George TRICE and my grandmother Louisa CREBER as the certificate will give me the bride's and groom's ages – hopefully - and their fathers' names.

Birth Certificates

This is what you would find on a birth certificate if you ordered one. However, do **not** rush off and order any certificates just yet. You do not always need a certificate to continue your research.

- **Registration District**
  This identifies the registration district of the event and will help when searching the census records.
- **Sub-District**
- **County**
  This will help when looking for other life events and parish registers.
- **Where and when born**
  This could be an address, church, or other place where the event took place.
- **Name and sex**
  Having the sex stated helps to identify males or females with old names. A name might not be on a birth certificate if it is thought the child might not survive or the parents have not thought of a name by registration!
- **Father's name**
  This might not be given on a birth certificate if child is illegitimate.
- **Mother's name**
  This will be her maiden name but if she had been married before, it will show her previous married name and should indicate a maiden name as well.
- **Father's occupation**
  Useful as evidence if unsure of a link to the individual
- **Informant**
  Name, address and possibly relationship to the individual
- **When registered**
  Should be within forty-two days of the event.

The following exercise will help you to use the FreeBMD website. When you have completed the exercise, check your answers with those at the back of the book.

Having had some practice using FreeBMD, you can then start on your own research.

Exercise 3

Using the FreeBMD website **find the birth registrations** for the following famous people.

1. **Sir Alfred Joseph Hitchcock KBE, the British-born American film director and producer, a master of the suspense thriller was born in Leytonstone, London on the 13 Aug 1899 and died in the USA on 29 Aprl 1980.**

    Year and quarter ....

    District.............................Vol....................Page........................

2. **Thomas Hardy, the British author, was born in 1840 in a hamlet called Higher Brockhampton in Dorset, three miles from the town of Dorchester.**

    Year and quarter ....

    District.............................Vol....................Page........................

3. **Born in Nottingham in 1850, Sir Jesse Boot transformed a small herbal store into a powerful pharmaceutical giant - *Boots the Chemist*.**

    Year and quarter ....

    District.............................Vol....................Page........................

4. **John James Sainsbury was born on 12 Jun 1844 at 5 Oakley Street, Lambeth. His first job was with a grocer in New Cut, Lambeth. After gaining experience with several other grocery businesses, he founded the *Sainsbury's* supermarket chain.**

    Year and quarter ....

    District.............................Vol....................Page........................

5. **William Gilbert Grace (18 Jul 1848 – 23 Oct 1915) was an English cricketer who, by his extraordinary skills, made cricket perhaps the first modern spectator sport, and who developed most of the techniques of modern batting.**

    Year and quarter ....

    District.............................Vol....................Page........................

6. **Neville (born Arthur Neville) Chamberlain was a British Conservative politician who served as Prime Minister from May 1937 to May 1940. He died in 1940 aged 71. He married Anne Cole and had two children, Francis and Dorothy.**

    Year and quarter ....

    District.............................Vol....................Page........................

Now find the birth registration details for his two children.

Name…………………………Year and quarter …………………………………..

District…………………………………Vol…………………Page…………………..

Name……………………………Year and quarter ………………………………..

District…………………………………Vol…………………Page…………………..

7. **Clement Richard Attlee was a British Labour politician who served as the Prime Minister of the United Kingdom from 1945 to 1951. He was born in Putney, London and married his wife Violet Millar in Hampstead London. They had four children - Janet Helen, Felicity Ann, Martin Richard and Alison Elizabeth. Clement Attlee died in October 1967 aged 84.**

Find his birth registration details

Year and quarter …………………………………..

District……………………………………Vol…………………Page……………………

Now find the birth registration details for his four children.

Name……………………………Year and quarter …………………………………

District……………………………………Vol…………………Page………………

Name……………………………Year and quarter …………………………………

District……………………………………Vol…………………Page………………

Name……………………………Year and quarter …………………………………..

District……………………………………Vol…………………Page………………..

Name……………………………Year and quarter …………………………………

District……………………………………Vol…………………Page………………..

8. **Margaret Hilda Thatcher served as Prime Minister of the United Kingdom from 1979 to 1990 and she is the first woman to have held this post. She was born Margaret Hilda Roberts on 13 Oct 1925 in Grantham to Alfred and Beatrice Ethel Roberts. She and her older sister Muriel were raised in the flat above the larger of the two located near the railway line.**

   Year and quarter …………………………..

   District……………………………….Vol…………………Page……………………

   Find her sister's birth registration details.

   Year and quarter …………………………..

   District……………………………….Vol…………………Page……………………

Chapter 3

Summary

This chapter will describe the civil registration process and explain how to obtain a life event certificate.

Civil Registration

Before 1837 churches and chapels recorded baptisms, marriages and burials. This information was held at a local level. In the early 1830s the coming of the railways and the Industrial Revolution meant that the Government needed to have some idea of population size and distribution, so changed the system.

Civil registration was first introduced with the Births and Deaths Registration Act 1836 which affected England and Wales. The General Register Office for England and Wales was responsible for the registration process. Civil registration of births, marriages, and deaths in England and Wales began on 1 July 1837 when registrars were expected to discover and record events. As a result your ancestors only had to supply information when asked. The Births and Deaths Act 1874 required those present at a birth or death to report the event.

Ireland began registration in 1845 for Protestant marriages. But it was 1864 before registration of all birth, marriage and death events. Civil registration was introduced in Scotland in 1855.

England and Wales

Births in England and Wales must be registered within forty-two days of the birth, whilst deaths must be registered within five days unless an inquest is called or a post-mortem is held.

Marriages are registered at the time of the ceremony by an officiating minister of the church, an authorised person at a registered building or a registrar at a register office, registered building or approved premise.

The general public do not have direct access to the official registers. Instead, indexes are made available which can be used to find the relevant register entry; then you can ask for a certified copy of the details.

The General Register Office has overall responsibility for registration administration.

Scotland

Civil registration came into force in Scotland on 1 January 1855. A significant difference from the English system is that far more detail is required for a registration. This means that if a certified copy of an entry is requested, it will contain more information than an English certificate.

The General Register Office for Scotland has overall responsibility for registration administration and drafting legislative changes in this area (as well as census data). They are governed by the Registration of Births, Deaths and Marriages (Scotland) Act 1965 and subsequent legislation.

Family Search website has a useful page on civil registration. Type the following link into our web browser.

www.familysearch.org/wiki/en/England_Civil_Registration

The National Archives website may be useful if you are looking for events at sea or abroad. Type the following link into our web browser.

www.nationalarchives.gov.uk/help-with-your-research/research-guides/birth-marriage-death-sea-or-abroad/

Overseas events

From 1849 if a person married, gave birth or died outside the British Empire or Commonwealth, the British Consul, *if informed*, would record the event and eventually pass the information to the general registrar's office. You can find these records on Findmypast, Ancestry and at the National Archives.

Obtaining the certificates

You can find a reference to these certificates, and you will need this reference to order a copy of the certificate, whether certified or not. The General Register Office holds copies of the registers and Local Register Offices hold the originals.

Short certificates were issued at the time of registration at no cost but did not contain the full details. If you wanted a long certificate with full details you had to pay for it.

When do I need registration certificates?

Certificates are expensive but we do not always need to obtain a copy as we will see when we continue the research of my family. Here is an example showing when you might need a certificate.

> **Example**
> Frederick TRICE aged eight in the 1871 census is shown as born in Pimlico. His mother is from Homburg Germany. BUT in the 1881 census Frederick is aged twenty born in Homburg Germany. Is this the Frederick in my family tree? To answer this question I need a birth certificate for Frederick which will give me the names of his parents.

The Local Register Office

The registration of births and deaths is undertaken at the local registrar's office by a member of the family. Sometimes births are registered at the hospital where the birth took place.

The local register offices periodically send a copy of all birth, marriage and death registrations to the General Register Office.

Why use the Local Register Office?

- You will get a copy of the original registration document IF the local register office scans the original.

- If the local register office scans the original, you will see the actual signatures of the bridal couple or the registrant.

- The copy sent to the GRO may have been illegible. Hopefully, the local register office copy will be better, especially if it is a scan of the original.

- The local register office has a different index with more information such as mother's maiden name. However, the GRO website index now includes this information.

If visiting a local register office, check to see if a fee is to be paid and whether they need warning of your planned visit.

Registration Districts

England and Wales was divided into Registration Districts with each having a unique code number.

Some important dates

1874 - Registration of a death requires a medical certificate of death. If an unmarried father's name is to appear on a birth certificate, he will have to be present at the registration of the birth.

1898 - Nonconformist places of worship permitted to conduct marriages

1926 - Births of illegitimate children can be registered retrospectively if the parents marry. Still births are registered.

1927 - Adoptions are registered.

The GRO Indexes

The GRO reference consists of the following information:

- The year of the event.
- The Year Quarter in which it took place
  - Jan, Feb, **MAR**
  - Apr, May, **JUN**
  - Jul, Aug, **SEPT**
  - Oct, Nov, **DEC**
- The district of the event
- Volume and page reference of the register.

Obtaining a certificate

Birth, marriage and death certificates can be ordered online from the GRO website.

Chapter five will explain how to use the website to search for a birth or death and how to order a certificate.

Do not order from any other website as it could cost you in excess of £25.

On the GRO website you will have to register with an email address and password. Payment is made by credit or debit card with the cost of a certified copy being £11. However, you can order an uncertified copy in PDF format for births and deaths for £7; note that some PDF copies may not show the column headings

But...?

What if you cannot find your ancestor's date of birth?

If your ancestor was born towards the *end* of a particular quarter, then the registered birth may be in the *next* quarter's index. If the event was in the last month of the year it might be registered in the first quarter of the next year. So always search at least one year either side of the expected date of the event.

If you are using an age given on the marriage certificate of the parent, can you be sure your ancestor was truthful? I know of a lady who contacted her employer to explain that when recruited she gave her age as five years younger than it was. She said she was now fifty-nine, not fifty-four, and would be due to retire soon.

If your ancestor was born between 1837 and 1875, the birth may not have been recorded because it was not until 1875 that it became mandatory to register these events. So you should look in parish registers for baptisms as an alternative as they continued to be recorded for parents who had their child baptised.

Chapter 4

Summary

This chapter will show you how to use FreeBMD to find a marriage or a death. There is a description of what you will find on a marriage and death certificate.

Searching for a marriage on the FreeBMD website

In chapter two we found several matches for my grandfather George TRICE. To help me find which entry relates to my ancestor, I decided to find his marriage to Louisa CREBER who I knew was my grandmother. If he was born in the 1870s, then I guessed he would have got married around the age of twenty in the 1890s.

Once again we will use FreeBMD. Go back to chapter two and follow steps 1 and 2. Then continue with this step-by-step guide.

1. This time choose **Marriage** as the **Type**.
2. If you only know the name of one of the couple then you can still find their marriage.
3. Just enter the groom's name or the bride's name. As you will see, you will find the names of the married couples.
4. Enter the **Surname** and **First name(s)** of the individual or the names of the couple.
5. If you enter only the name of one of the couple, you will get a list of matches to that name. You will need to select the marriage by knowing the district of the marriage.
6. If you know the first name of the other spouse then this will reduce the number of matches.
7. I entered George TRICE and the first name of my grandmother - Louisa.
8. In the **Date range** enter 1890 to 1899.
9. The screen should like this if you are following the guide.

			Districts	All Districts
	☐ All			Aberayron (to Jun1936)
	☐ Births	Help		Aberconwy (from Sep1975)
Type	☐ Deaths	Click for help		Abergavenny (to 1958)
		on using FreeBMD		Aberystwyth (to Jun1936)
	☑ Marriages			Abingdon
				Acle (1939-Mar1974)
Surname	Trice			Alcester (to Sep1985)
				Alderbury (to Jun1895)
First name(s)	George			Aldershot (Dec1932-Mar1974)
Spouse/Mother surname				Aldridge & Brownhills (Jun1966-Mar1974)
				Aled (Dec1935-Mar1974)
Spouse first name(s)	Louisa			Alnwick (to 1936)
Death age/DoB				Alresford (to Sep1932)
Date range	Mar ⌄ 1890 to Dec ⌄ 1899			
Volume/Page	/		Counties	All Counties
				Anglesey (to Mar1974)
	☐ Mono			Avon (from Jun1974)
				Bedfordshire
Options	☐ Exact match on first names			Berkshire
	☐ Phonetic search surnames			Breconshire (to Mar1974)

10. Click the red **Find** button at the bottom of the screen.

11. This is part of the displayed web page.

Search for   *Type:* Marriages   *Surname:* Trice
         Start date: Mar 1890   *End date:* Dec

Whilst FreeBMD makes every effort to ensure accurate trans...
an entry has the symbol 👓 next to it you can view the scan of

If you are SURE that our transcription(s) below differs from ...

Surname First name(s) District Vol Page

Marriages Mar 1894 (>99%)

| Trice | George James | W. Ham | 4a | 183 | [Info] 👓 |

Marriages Mar 1896 (>99%)

| Trice | George | Stoke D | 5b | 467 | [Info] 👓 |

12. I was lucky as there were only two matches. But as you can see there is no information about his wife.
13. Refer to chapter two for an explanation of the **District** name in blue and the **Info** and **spectacles** icons.
14. My father was born in Plymouth and checking the district details I discovered that Stoke D is in Devon. This looked a likely match.
15. If you click on the blue page number it will show you the couples who are recorded.

Search for   *Type:* Marriages   *Start date:* Mar
         Volume: 5b   *Page:* 467

Whilst FreeBMD makes every effort to ensure accurate tran...
certificate. If an entry has the symbol 👓 next to it you can v

If you are SURE that our transcription(s) below differs from

Surname First name(s) District Vol Page

Marriages Mar 1896 (>99%)

Creber	Louisa	Stoke D	5b	467	[Info] 👓
Retallick	Elizabeth	Stoke D.	5b	467	[Info] 👓
Sloman	John Henry	Stoke D.	5b	467	[Info] 👓
Trice	George	Stoke D.	5b	467	[Info] 👓

16. This display shows two men and two women.
17. Having established that George and Louisa married in Stoke D, which is now an area in Plymouth, I could now look for the couple in the 1901 census.
18. But what if you did not know the name of one of the couple? You would have to search for a George TRICE married to a Louisa or to an Elizabeth in the 1901 census.
19. Hopefully you only find one possible match.

Marriage and Death Certificates

This is the information you will find on a marriage or death certificate.

- **Where and when married or died**

  This could be an address, church, or other place where the event took place.

- **Name and sex**

  The sex is only given on the death certificate.   Sometimes it is difficult to identify male or female with old names.

- **Bride's and groom's condition**

  This will be spinster, bachelor, widow or widower on a marriage certificate.

- **Ages**

  Their ages are given on a marriage certificate but sometimes it will state *of full age* which implies being over the legal age for a marriage. On a death certificate the age at death is given from 1866 and the date of birth is given from 1969.

- **Banns or Licence**

  This shows if the marriage follows banns being called or a licence issued if married in a church. A superintendent's certificate is issued if married at a register office.

- **Father's name**

  Fathers of the bride and groom are named. Not on a death certificate.

- **Father's occupation**

  This is useful as evidence if unsure of a link to the individual. On a death certificate it will be the last known occupation.   For a wife, the certificate may give details of husband's occupation and his address.

- **Informant**

  Name, address and possible relationship to the individual will be on a death certificate. It might be a coroner's registration of a death which would indicate an inquest had been held.

- **Date of registration**

However, **do not** rush off and order any certificates just yet. You do not always need a certificate to continue your research.

If you obtained a marriage certificate, you will see if the married couple signed the certificate or if they signed with their mark. Names of the witnesses will be given. Who are they? Are they related to the married couple?

If it is a civil marriage, then a notice of intent to marry had to be displayed at the register office in the district in which the couple had been resident for at least a week. If they are living in two different districts, both register offices needed to display the notice.

Prior to 1852, up to four marriages were entered on each page of the register. After that (with a few exceptions) there were two marriages per page. Each page of the register is identified by the district, volume and page.

So searching for a marriage between 1837 and 1852 will result in seeing eight people listed. Searching for a marriage after 1852 will result in just four people listed. But looking at the index and the four or eight names listed, you will not be able to tell who married whom! So your next step is to check the census immediately after the marriage. If you gain no further information or confirmation of who married whom, then the only option is to buy the marriage certificate from the GRO.

Searching for a death on the FreeBMD website

While we are looking at FreeBMD we will take this opportunity to search for the death of George TRICE. My father had told me he died in the 1940s.

Go back to chapter two and follow steps 1 and 2. Then continue with this step-by-step guide.

1. This time choose death as the **Type**.
2. Enter the **Surname** and **First name(s)** of the individual.
3. I entered George TRICE.
4. Then in the **Date range** enter 1940 to 1949.
5. Click the red **Find** button at the bottom of the screen.

If you are SURE that our transcription(s) below differs from the GRC

Surname	First name(s)	Age	District	Vol	Page		

Deaths Mar 1944 (>99%)

Trice	George	71	Penzance	5c	298	Info	𝒪

Deaths Jun 1944 (>99%)

Trice	George	68	Tonbridge	2a	1197	Info	𝒪

6. I found two possible references - one in Cornwall and one in Kent.
7. The ages did not help me but I did have a photo of my grandparents outside a cottage in Marazion, Cornwall taken in the 1940s.
8. So my grandfather's death was registered in March 1944. Of course, he might have actually died in late 1943 or in the first three months of 1944.
9. If his age was correctly given as 71, then he was born in 1872 or 1873.

So what have we found so far? My grandfather's marriage to Louisa CREBER was registered in March 1896, so they could have married in late 1895 or early 1896.

I also know that he died in late 1943 or early 1944. But I still do not know where he was born.

> **Remember**
> The ages and names may not be accurate on either the marriage or death certificate.
>
> I have a death certificate registered by a coroner which gives the incorrect name of the deceased.
>
> On a marriage certificate if the bride was older than the groom, she might give her age as younger than his.

What if you cannot find your ancestor's date of marriage or death?

- If they died between 1837 and 1875 the event may not have been recorded, so look in parish registers for a burial.
- If your ancestor was married or died towards the end of a particular quarter, then the registered marriage or death may be in the next quarter's index.

Exercise 4

Using the FreeBMD website, complete the details below.

1. **Neville (born Arthur Neville) Chamberlain was a British Conservative politician who served as Prime Minister from May 1937 to May 1940.   He died in 1940 aged 71.   He married Anne Cole.**

   Find his **marriage** registration details.

   Year and quarter ....
   District.. Vol........................ Page...............................

   Find his **death** registration details.

   Year and quarter ....
   District.. Vol........................ Page...............................

2. **Karl Marx was born in the city of Trier, Germany. Marx was a revolutionary and the co-originator of *The Communist Manifesto*. On 14 Mar 1883, Marx passed away peacefully in his armchair. He lies buried at Highgate Cemetery in London.**

   Find his **death** registration details.

   Year and quarter .... Age at death...........................
   District.. Vol........................ Page...............................

3. **In about 1908 Clementine Ogilvy Hozier married a famous politician.**

   Find her **marriage** registration details.

   Name of spouse..
   Year and quarter ....
   District.. Vol........................ Page...............................

4. **Emmeline Pankhurst (1858 - 1928), better known as Emily Pankhurst, founded the Women's Social and Political Union and worked throughout her life for the cause of women's suffrage. In 1879 she married Richard Pankhurst.**

   Find her **marriage** registration details.

   Her maiden name ....
   Year and quarter ....
   District.. Vol........................ Page...............................

5. **Maria Dickin CBE (1870 - 1951) was an animal welfare pioneer who founded the PDSA in 1917. At the age of twenty-eight she married her first cousin.**

   Find her **marriage** registration details.

   Her spouse's name ....
   Year and quarter ....
   District............................
   .... Vol........................   Page............................

6. **Charles Babbage was an English mathematician, analytical philosopher, mechanical engineer scientist who originated the idea of a programmable computer. He died in approx 1871.**

   Find his **death** registration details.

   Year and quarter ....   Age at death............................
   District.. Vol........................   Page............................

7. **Margaret Hilda Thatcher served as Prime Minister of the United Kingdom from 1979 to 1990 and she was the first woman to have held this post. She was born Margaret Hilda Roberts on 13 Oct 1925 in Grantham to Alfred and Beatrice Ethel Roberts.**

   Find her parents' **marriage** registration details.

   Year and quarter ....
   District.. Vol........................   Page............................

8. **Clement Richard Attlee was a British Labour politician who served as the Prime Minister of the United Kingdom from 1945 to 1951. He was born in Putney, London and married his wife Violet Millar in Hampstead London. Clement Attlee died in October 1967 aged 84.**

   Find his **marriage** registration details.

   Year and quarter ....
   District.. Vol........................   Page............................

   Find his **death** registration details.

   Year and quarter ....   Age at death............................
   District.. Vol........................   Page............................

·Chapter 5

Summary

This chapter will show you how to search for a birth or death using the GRO index. The way to order a copy certificate is also covered. The GRO site is useful as the mother's maiden name is often given for births.

The General Register Office - GRO

The GRO holds copies of the birth, marriage and death records for England and Wales from 1837. The birth records show the maiden name of the mother and the death records will show the age at death. The GRO online index is updated annually by one year. If the woman has been married before, her previous married and maiden names should be given on the certificate. If you want a marriage certificate, you will have to choose the **Place an Order** option on the GRO website. [Prices shown below are correct at 2023.]

Please note - you cannot search the marriage index on the GRO website so you will need the GRO reference from a site such as FreeBMD.

How to access and use the GRO website

1.   Type www.gro.gov.uk/gro/content into your web browser and this screen will appear.

General Register Office
Official information on births, adoptions, marriages, civil partnerships and deaths in England and Wales

The **General Register Office** is part of **Her Majesty's Passport Office** and oversees civil registration in England and Wales. We maintain the national archive of all births, marriages and deaths dating back to 1837 and further information on our services can be found using the links shown below.

▸ **Order certificates online**
from the General Register Office

It's quick and easy to order birth, marriage, civil partnership, death, adoption and commemorative certificates online via the government's own official website.

Certificates cost from £11.00 including postage. In a hurry? Use the priority service from £35.00

The General Register Office

Know your ancestors better

Certificates bring your search to life with unique and sometimes unexpected information about your ancestors

Get certificates from just £11.00 direct from the General Register Office, the official source of birth, marriage & death certificates for the whole of England and Wales since 1837

Order certificates online at www.gro.gov.uk

▸ **Apply online for a UK Passport**
You can apply for, renew, replace or update your passport and pay for it online

2.   Even if you just want to browse the indexes, you must click on **Order certificates online**.
3.   Scroll down on the next screen where you have to register or login. This costs you nothing.

Service Information

This service requires your browser to accept cookies - please see our Cookie Policy for more information.

This service does not support the use of the browser BACK button, please only use links and button options to navigate the site.

Service Updates

Due to current high demand, some customers may experience a delay in receiving their order. If you need to contact us please do so using the online form that can be found on GOV.UK or email us at certificate.services@gro.gov.uk.

For orders using Royal Mail or DHL Delivery, please check their websites for current information about disruption within their postal services.

Register or Login

E-Mail address [   ]   [Login] [Reset]

Password [   ]

Forgotten your password?
Need to change your details?

If you are using the site for the first time you will need to complete the registration process:
Register as an Individual
Register as a representative of a Company or Organisation

4. Once you have registered, just enter your email address and your chosen password and click the **Login** button.

5. You will then see the screen shown below giving you various options.

6. Click on **Search the GRO indexes** to display this screen.

7. Now you can start searching for a birth or death registration reference.

Searching the GRO website for a birth record

1. When you can see this screen click on the **Birth** option.

2. Enter the year of birth and you can search two years either side of this date from the drop-down box.

3. The dates covered for births are from 1837 to 1934 and from 1984 to 2021. Searching for George TRICE born in the 1870s, I selected a date of 1872 with +/- two years. This gives a range of 1870 to 1874.

4. On the next page, part of the website screen is shown with those details entered.

⊙ Birth   ○ Death

When was the birth registered?
Year:* ❓   1872 ▾ +/- 2 ▾ year(s) ❓

Please enter your search criteria, mandatory fields are indicated with a *
Up to 250 matching results will be returned so providing any additional information you
know will help locate the registration you are looking for.

Who are you searching for?

Surname at Birth:*	Trice ⓥ ❓	Include:	Exact Matches Only ▾ ❓

Search for records with a matching surname

First Forename:	George ❓	Include:	Exact Matches Only ▾ ❓

Search for records with a matching first forename

Second Forename:	❓
Sex:*	Male ▾ ❓

Mother's Maiden Surname:	ⓥ ❓	Include:	Exact Matches Only ▾ ❓

Search for records with a matching Mother's Maiden Surname

Where was the birth registered?
District of Birth: ❓

Do you already know any GRO Reference details for the registration?
Quarter: Select ▾ ❓
Volume: ❓   Page: ❓

Search   Reset

5. You must complete all the fields with a red star. These are year, surname and sex. I have added the first name although this is not mandatory.
6. Then click the blue **Search** button to display this screen. You may need to scroll down the screen to see the selected records.

Search   Reset

Results: ❓

Select the button by an individual result to see ordering options available for that record.

	Name:	Mother's Maiden Surname:
○	**TRICE, GEORGE** *GRO Reference:* 1871 M Quarter in BRIGHTON Volume 02B Page 260	**SCHRAMN**
○	**TRICE, GEORGE FREDERICK** *GRO Reference:* 1871 M Quarter in THANET Volume 02A Page 814	-
○	**TRICE, GEORGE THOMAS** *GRO Reference:* 1871 J Quarter in PORTSEA ISLAND Volume 02B Page 453	**BUTTON**
○	**TRICE, GEORGE WILLIAM** *GRO Reference:* 1870 S Quarter in EAST ASHFORD Volume 02A Page 665	**PANTENEY**
○	**TRICE, GEORGE WILLIAM** *GRO Reference:* 1872 M Quarter in SHEPPEY Volume 02A Page 810	**ATKINS**
○	**TRICE, GEORGE WILLIAM VALENTINE** *GRO Reference:* 1874 M Quarter in ELHAM Volume 02A Page 923	**DOWN**

6 Record(s) Found - Showing Page 1 of 1
Go to page 1

7. This matches the list we found with the FreeBMD search but with the addition of the maiden name of each child's mother, where known.
8. Choose the relevant record you are looking for based on the expected maiden name of the mother [if known] and the place of birth if known.
9. Below each name is the GRO reference to year, quarter, district and volume and page numbers.

Searching the GRO website for a death record

1. When you can see this screen click the **Death** option.

HM Passport Office

General Register Office
Official information on births, adoptions, marriages, civil partnerships and deaths in England and Wales

Search the GRO Online Indexes

Which index would you like to search?
Events registered in England or Wales:

○ Birth   ○ Death

Home > Online Ordering

© 2022 Crown Copyright
Accessibility | Copyright | Terms and Conditions | Privacy Statement | Cookie Policy - Revoke Consent | GOV.UK
Site Version: V284-LH2 | Date Last Updated: 09/06/2022

- Logout
- Main Menu
- Place an Order
- Search the GRO Online Index
- Data Quality & Error Reporting
- My Details
- My Orders
- Frequently Asked Questions
- Contact us
- View GRO information on GOV.UK
- Births & Adoptions
- Marriage & Civil Partnership
- Death
- Family History Records
- Cookie Policy
- Apply online for a UK Passport

2. Enter the year of death and you can search two years either side of this date from the drop-down box.

HM Passport Office

General Register Office
Official information on births, adoptions, marriages, civil partnerships and deaths in England and Wales

Search the GRO Online Indexes

Which index would you like to search?
Events registered in England or Wales:

○ Birth   ◉ Death

When was the death registered?
Year:* ❔   [Select ▾] +/- [0 ▾] year(s) ❔

Home > Online Ordering

© 2022 Crown Copyright
Accessibility | Copyright | Terms and Conditions | Privacy Statement | Cookie Policy - Revoke Consent | GOV.UK
Site Version: V284-LH2 | Date Last Updated: 09/06/2022

- Logout
- Main Menu
- Place an Order
- Search the GRO Online Index
- Data Quality & Error Reporting
- My Details
- My Orders
- Frequently Asked Questions
- Contact us
- View GRO information on GOV.UK
- Births & Adoptions
- Marriage & Civil Partnership
- Death
- Family History Records
- Cookie Policy
- Apply online for a UK Passport

3. The dates covered for deaths are from 1837 to 1957 and from 1984 to 2021.
4. Searching for George TRICE who died in the 1940s, I selected a date of 1942 with +/- two years. This gives a range of 1940 to 1944.
5. The next screen shows part of the website page with those details.

○ Birth   ● Death

When was the death registered?
Year:* ❓   [1942 ▾] +/- [2 ▾] year(s) ❓

Please enter your search criteria, mandatory fields are indicated with a *
Up to 250 matching results will be returned so providing any additional information you
know will help locate the registration you are looking for.

Who are you searching for?

Surname at
Death:*   [Trice ⬇] ❓   Include: [Exact Matches Only ▾]
                                          ❓

Search for records with a matching surname

First
Forename at   [George]   ❓   Include: [Exact Matches Only ▾]
Death: ❓

Search for records with a matching first forename

Second
Forename at   [   ] ❓
Death:

                                Age at
                                Death   [   ] ❓ _ +/- [0 ▾] year(s) ❓
Sex:*   [Male   ▾] ❓ in   *(Enter 0 if less than 1 year old)*
                                years:

Where was the death registered?
District of
Death: [   ] ❓

Do you already know any GRO Reference details for the registration?
Quarter: [Select   ▾] ❓
Volume: [   ] ❓   Page: [   ] ❓

[Search]   [Reset]

6. You must complete all the fields with a red star. These are year, surname and sex. I have added the first name although this is not mandatory.
7. Then click the blue **Search** button to display this list of possible matches. You may need to scroll down the screen to see the selected records.

[Search]   [Reset]

Results: ❓

Select the button by an individual result to see ordering options available
for that record.

Name:	Age at Death (in years):
○ TRICE, GEORGE *GRO Reference:* 1944 M Quarter in PENZANCE Volume 05C Page 298	71
○ TRICE, GEORGE *GRO Reference:* 1944 J Quarter in TONBRIDGE Volume 02A Page 1197	68

2 Record(s) Found - Showing Page 1 of 1
Go to page [1]

8. This matches the list we found with FreeBMD including the age at death.
9. Choose the relevant record you are looking for based on the age at death and possible place of death if known.
10. Below each name is the GRO reference to year, quarter, district and volume and page numbers.

Ordering a certificate from the GRO website

1. Once you have found the relevant birth or death record you can order a certificate.
2. The process is the same whether you are ordering a birth or death certificate.
3. If you remember we found a death registration for George Trice in 1944.

Results: ?

Select the button by an individual result to see ordering options available for that record.

	Name:	Age at Death (in years):
○	**TRICE, GEORGE** *GRO Reference:* 1944 M Quarter in PENZANCE Volume 05C Page 298	71
○	**TRICE, GEORGE** *GRO Reference:* 1944 J Quarter in TONBRIDGE Volume 02A Page 1197	68

2 Record(s) Found - Showing Page 1 of 1
Go to page 1

4. As I knew that George Trice had lived in Cornwall, the Penzance registration is the correct record.
5. Click the open circle beside the GRO reference for which you want a copy and two blue buttons appear as shown below.

Results: ?

Select the button by an individual result to see ordering options available for that record.

	Name:	Age at Death (in years):
◉	**TRICE, GEORGE** *GRO Reference:* 1944 M Quarter in PENZANCE Volume 05C Page 298 **Order this entry as a:** `Certificate` `PDF`	71
○	**TRICE, GEORGE** *GRO Reference:* 1944 J Quarter in TONBRIDGE Volume 02A Page 1197	68

2 Record(s) Found - Showing Page 1 of 1
Go to page 1

6. The blue buttons are labelled **Certificate** and **PDF**.
7. Choose which one you want. The certificate option will provide you with a certified copy through the post whereas a PDF provides the information in a document sent to you by email and is cheaper. Note that as of 2023, PDF copies are available pre-1957 for deaths and pre-1920 for births. Later dates are available as certified copies only.
8. In this case I chose the certificate option. On the next page is the screen you will see; it is a long one, so I have copied it as several images.

Application for an England and Wales Death registration record

Below is an England and Wales Death Registration Record Application Form.

PDF copies of the entry are only available for the digitised entries for the years 1837-1957 and where a GRO reference is supplied, which you can find using the GRO Online Historical Indexes.

Required fields will be followed by the * character.

Please complete the form and press the "Submit" button to add the application to your basket.

Details of the person in the entry required

Year death was registered	1944
Surname of deceased *	TRICE
Forenames of deceased *	GEORGE

Reference information from GRO Index

Year	1944
Quarter*	Jan, Feb, Mar
District name*	PENZANCE
Volume Number*	05C
Page Number*	298

9. The website automatically enters the registration reference as shown above.
10. The next screen is where you choose the **Delivery Method**. You can change your mind and choose the PDF option shown at the bottom of the screen.

Service Options

Please choose the item type, service and delivery method you require:

Certificate	⦿ Standard - £11.00, despatched on the 4th working day from receipt of order.
	○ Priority - £35.00, despatched next working day from receipt of order.
Delivery Method:	Post ⌄

Post - 1st Class (Priority) and 2nd Class (Standard) for UK address, Airmail outside UK

Royal Mail Next Working Day - Priority applications sent to UK addresses Only (+£7.25 per batch of up to 5 Certificates)

Royal Mail Saturday 9am - Priority applications sent to UK addresses Only (+£19.25 per batch of up to 5 Certificates)

For Royal Mail Saturday 9am delivery, orders must be made before 4pm on a Thursday.

DHL - Priority applications sent to Addresses outside the UK Only, DHL are unable to deliver to PO BOX address (+£12 per batch of up to 5 Certificates)

PDF copy of the entry	○ Standard - £7.00, despatched on the 4th working day from receipt of order.
Delivery Method:	Uploaded to be viewed via My Orders page (deleted after 3 months)

11.   You can increase the number of copies here.

The cut off time for orders is 16:00 hrs. Applications received after this time will result in the order date being that of the next working day.

Please note that orders received, on Saturday or Sunday, will be classed as received on Monday (except those received on Bank Holidays, which will be classed as received on the following working day).

Quantity: *   [1]   Full

Please note additional copies of certificates will be charged at £11.00 on the standard service and £35.00 on the Priority Service. Quantity should always be 1 for PDF applications.

Please type your personal reference for this application:

Your reference   [_____]

[Submit] [Reset]

12.   If you wish, you can add your own reference but this is optional.
13.   On the bottom of this screen click the blue **Submit** button.
14.   On the next screen you will be asked to enter your delivery address details. Once you have ordered something, GRO saves those details, but you will be asked to check and amend, if necessary, the next time you order.
15.   Then click the **Submit** button at the foot of the screen.
16.   Then you will be shown a summary of your order as shown below.

The table below contains summary details of all applications currently in your basket.

Each row in the table represents an individual application.

Please use the buttons at the bottom of the table to 'checkout' or to continue with your order. The buttons to the right of each application row can be used to delete or edit an individual application.

If you wish to assign a reference number to the order then please enter this at the top of the form and click the button marked ' Set Ref ' to do so.

Order Reference [_____] [Set Ref]

Name	Item Type	Quantity	Delivery Method	Despatch Date (Est)	Customer Ref	Price	Actions
GEORGE TRICE	E/W Death Certificate	1	Post - 2nd Class or Airmail	19 Oct 2022		£11.00	[Edit] [Delete]

Year	Qtr	District	Vol	Page	Reg	Ent	NoDOR
1944	Mar	PENZANCE	05C	298			

Shipping Method Summary

Shipping Method	Quantity	Total
Post - 2nd Class or Airmail	1 at £0.00	£0.00
	Shipping Total:	£0.00

Order Total: £11.00

Please note: Delivery time should be added to the stated despatch date to calculate when your order should reach you.

[Checkout] [Continue Shopping] [Return to the GRO Indexes]

17.   There are three blue buttons labelled **Checkout**, **Continue Shopping** or **Return to GRO Indexes**.

18. If you go to **Checkout,** you will be asked for details of your payment method.

Proceed with payment

Return to basket

Do not use the browser back button to return.
If you wish to return to your basket now then please click the 'Return to basket' or 'Go Back' buttons.

Please check the contents of your basket and then click 'Confirm' to proceed with payment. You will be allowed 15 minutes to complete the process.

Name	Item Type	Quantity	Delivery Method	Despatch Date (Est)	Customer Ref	Price
GEORGE TRICE	E/W Death Certificate	1	Post - 2nd Class or Airmail	19 Oct 2022		£11.00

Year	Qtr	District	Vol	Page	Reg	Ent	NoDOR
1944	Mar	PENZANCE	05C	298			

Shipping Method Summary

Shipping Method	Quantity	Total
Post - 2nd Class or Airmail	1 at £0.00	£0.00
	Shipping Total:	£0.00

Order Total:
£11.00

Please note: Mail delivery time should be added to the stated despatch date to calculate when your order should reach you.

ORDERS CAN NOT BE AMENDED OR CANCELLED ONCE THE ORDER HAS BEEN BOOKED. THIS INCLUDES DELIVERY ADDRESS, SHIPPING UPGRADES AND CERTIFICATE INFORMATION. PLEASE ENSURE ALL INFORMATION IS CORRECT BEFORE COMPLETING PURCHASE.

GO BACK   CONFIRM

19. If the details are not correct, then click the blue **Go Back** button to amend the details. Otherwise click the blue **Confirm** button and the **Secure Payment Page** will display.
20. Otherwide click the blue **Confirm** button and the **Secure Payment Page** will display.

worldpay
from FIS

Help   FAQs   Security

Secure Payment Page

This payment page has been created by WorldPay for GRO Payment. Please review your purchase details, then select a card or payment to proceed to the next page.

Select language   English ⌄ ◗
GRO Payment
Description   GRO Basket
Amount   £11.00

Select your payment method   ◗

Mastercard   VISA   Maestro
Mastercard   Visa   Maestro

Cancel ⊗

worldpay from FIS   For help with your payment visit the: WorldPay from FIS Help.

© 2008 WorldPay Limited

21. Choose how you want to pay.
22. Once you have completed your order, you should be returned to the GRO website.
23. Once you have completed your order, click the **Logout** option on the top right-hand side of the screen.

Ordering a marriage certificate on the GRO website

1. If you are going to order a marriage certificate you will need the GRO index reference found on a website such as FreeBMD.
2. In your web browser type www.gro.gov.uk/gro/content and this screen will appear.

3. Click on **Order certificates online**.
4. On the next screen you will have to sign in if registered or register as an individual.

5. Once registered you will need to enter your email address and your chosen password and click the **Login** button.
6. You will then see the screen shown on the next page giving you various options.

HM Passport Office — **General Register Office**
Official information on births, adoptions, marriages, civil partnerships and deaths in England and Wales

What would you like to do?

Order a Certificate or PDF
Enter your details or a GRO Reference to order:
- A paper certificate that can be used for identification or official purposes
- A PDF copy of a record, not for official use

Search the GRO Indexes
Search the indexes to identify the record you want.

You can order a Certificate or PDF.

Find out more about
What we do and what records we hold.

Researching your family history and how to get the most out of the GRO records.

View recent orders
Check details and progress of your recent orders.

View and download your PDFs.

Check or update my details
Update contact and account details.

- Logout
- Main Menu
- Place an Order
- Search the GRO Online Index
- Data Quality & Error Reporting
- My Details
- My Orders
- Frequently Asked Questions
- Contact us
- View GRO information on GOV.UK
- Births & Adoptions
- Marriage & Civil Partnership
- Death
- Family History Records
- Cookie Policy
- Apply online for a UK Passport

7. Click on **Order a Certificate or PDF** to display this screen.

HM Passport Office — **General Register Office**
Official information on births, adoptions, marriages, civil partnerships and deaths in England and Wales

Start Application

Please choose from the following options to access the appropriate application form for ordering a certificate or PDF of the life event record you wish to order.

Applications for events registered within the last 6 months (for marriages this period is extended to 18 months) cannot be made via this site. This certificate ordering restriction does not apply to adoption certificates. After an adoption is registered at the General Register Office, you can apply on line for a full certificate.

N.B. This service does not support the use of the browser BACK button, please only use links and button options to navigate the site.

- Logout
- Main Menu
- Place an Order
- Search the GRO Online Index
- Data Quality & Error Reporting
- My Details
- My Orders
- Frequently Asked Questions
- Contact us
- View GRO information on GOV.UK
- Births & Adoptions
- Marriage & Civil Partnership
- Death
- Family History Records
- Cookie Policy
- Apply online for a UK Passport

Where was the event registered?

○ England or Wales

○ Another part of the United Kingdom or British Isles

○ Outside the United Kingdom and registered by the British Forces, Consul or High Commission

(including Forces or Regimental records in the UK, Ireland or other British Isles between 1761-1924, see **Overseas records GRO hold**)

8. Choose where the event was registered by clicking one of the open circles on this display.
9. Options 2 and 3 show you where to contact for events outside of England and Wales.
10. If you click the first option – **England or Wales** – then other options appear.
11. Select **Marriage** as the type of event as shown on the next page.

Where was the event registered?

◉ England or Wales

○ Another part of the United Kingdom or British Isles

○ Outside the United Kingdom and registered by the British Forces, Consul or High Commission

(including Forces or Regimental records in the UK, Ireland or other British Isles between 1761-1924, see **Overseas records GRO hold**)

What type of event was it?

○ Birth

○ Adoption *(A certificate in the post adoption name)*

◉ Marriage

12. Scroll down to the part which asks you for the year of the event.

When was the event registered?

1896 **Year** in which the event was registered

(If you don't know the exact date we can search the year you specify plus the year before and the year after for a matching registration)

How can the event be identified?

○ I know the **GRO Index Reference**

○ I want GRO to search for the registration and will provide details to identify it

(see **If I don't have the index reference what will happen?**)

13. I entered 1896 as the year of the marriage and then clicked **I know the GRO Index Reference** option. A new screen of information will be displayed and this is shown on the next page.

Application for an England and Wales Marriage registration record

Below is an England and Wales Marriage Registration Record Application Form where full information is required.

Required fields will be followed by the * character.

Please complete the form and press the "Submit" button to add the application to your basket.

Particulars of the couple in the entry required

A minimum of one name and forename for the same party must be given

Year marriage was registered	1896
Party 1 Surname	[_____]
Party 1 Forenames	[_____]
Party 2 Surname	[_____]
Party 2 Forenames	[_____]

Reference information from GRO Index

Year	1896
Quarter*	Select ⌄
District name*	[_____]
Volume Number*	[_____]
Page Number*	[_____]

If the index is incorrect and GRO are unable to locate an entry a refund will be provided minus a £3.50 administration fee.

14. On this screen enter a **Surname** and **Forename** of one of the couple who got married.

15. From the reference you obtained from the FreeBMD website enter Stoke D for the **District** and then 5b for the **Volume Number** and 467 for the **Page Number**.

16. This is shown below.

Application for an England and Wales Marriage registration record

Below is an England and Wales Marriage Registration Record Application Form where full information is required.

Required fields will be followed by the * character.

Please complete the form and press the "Submit" button to add the application to your basket.

Particulars of the couple in the entry required

A minimum of one name and forename for the same party must be given

Year marriage was registered	1896
Party 1 Surname	Trice
Party 1 Forenames	George
Party 2 Surname	[_____]
Party 2 Forenames	[_____]

Reference information from GRO Index

Year	1896
Quarter*	Jan, Feb, Mar ⌄
District name*	Stoke D
Volume Number*	5b
Page Number*	467

If the index is incorrect and GRO are unable to locate an entry a refund will be provided minus a £3.50 administration fee.

17. You need to scroll down to see the next part of the screen.

Volume Number*   5b

Page Number*   467

If the index is incorrect and GRO are unable to locate an entry a refund will be provided minus a £3.50 administration fee.

Service Options

Please choose the item type, service and delivery method you require:

Certificate   ◉ Standard - £11.00, despatched on the 4th working day from receipt of order.
○ Priority - £35.00, despatched next working day from receipt of order.

Delivery Method: Post

Post - 1st Class (Priority) and 2nd Class (Standard) for UK address, Airmail outside UK

Royal Mail Next Working Day - Priority applications sent to UK addresses Only (+£7.25 per batch of up to 5 Certificates)

Royal Mail Saturday 9am - Priority applications sent to UK addresses Only (+£19.25 per batch of up to 5 Certificates)

For Royal Mail Saturday 9am delivery, orders must be made before 4pm on a Thursday.

DHL - Priority applications sent to Addresses outside the UK Only, DHL are unable to deliver to PO BOX address (+£12 per batch of up to 5 Certificates)

18. The standard fee is applied and you can choose the delivery method which will be just **Post** unless you want a priority delivery.

Delivery Method: Post

Post - 1st Class (Priority) and 2nd Class (Standard) for UK address, Airmail outside UK

Royal Mail Next Working Day - Priority applications sent to UK addresses Only (+£7.25 per batch of up to 5 Certificates)

Royal Mail Saturday 9am - Priority applications sent to UK addresses Only (+£19.25 per batch of up to 5 Certificates)

For Royal Mail Saturday 9am delivery, orders must be made before 4pm on a Thursday.

DHL - Priority applications sent to Addresses outside the UK Only, DHL are unable to deliver to PO BOX address (+£12 per batch of up to 5 Certificates)

The cut off time for orders is 16:00 hrs. Applications received after this time will result in the order date being that of the next working day.

Please note that orders received, on Saturday or Sunday, will be classed as received on Monday (except those received on Bank Holidays, which will be classed as received on the following working day).

Quantity:*   1   Full

Please note additional copies of certificates will be charged at £11.00 on the standard service and £35.00 on the Priority Service.

Please type your personal reference for this application:

Your reference

Submit   Reset

19. Then choose how many copies you want and if you want to provide a reference of your own choosing before clicking the blue **Submit** button.
20. On the next screen you will be asked to enter your delivery address details. Once you have ordered something you will be asked to check and amend, if necessary, next time you order.
21. Then click the blue **Submit** button at the foot of the screen.

22.   Then you will be shown a summary of your order as shown below.

Basket Summary

The table below contains summary details of all applications currently in your basket.

Each row in the table represents an individual application.

Please use the buttons at the bottom of the table to 'checkout' or to continue with your order. The buttons to the right of each application row can be used to delete or edit an individual application.

If you wish to assign a reference number to the order then please enter this at the top of the form and click the button marked ' Set Ref ' to do so.

Order Reference [   ] [Set Ref]

Name	Item Type	Quantity	Delivery Method	Despatch Date (Est)	Customer Ref	Price	Actions	
George Trice	E/W Marriage Certificate	1	Post - 2nd Class or Airmail	19 Oct 2022		£11.00	Edit	Delete

Year	Qtr	District	Vol	Page	Reg	Ent	NoDOR
1896	Mar	Stoke D	5b	467			

Shipping Method Summary		
Shipping Method	Quantity	Total
Post - 2nd Class or Airmail	1 at £0.00	£0.00
	Shipping Total:	£0.00

Order Total: £11.00

Please note: Delivery time should be added to the stated despatch date to calculate when your order should reach you.

[Checkout]   [Continue Shopping]   [Search the GRO Indexes]

23.   At the foot of the summary there are three blue buttons which allow you to choose to **Checkout, Continue Shopping** or **Return to GRO Indexes**.

24.   Click the blue **Checkout** button and you will be asked for details of your payment method on the screen shown on the next page.

Proceed with payment

Return to basket

Do not use the browser back button to return.
If you wish to return to your basket now then please click the 'Return to basket' or 'Go Back' buttons.

Please check the contents of your basket and then click 'Confirm' to proceed with payment. You will be allowed 15 minutes to complete the process.

Name	Item Type	Quantity	Delivery Method	Despatch Date (Est)	Customer Ref	Price
George Trice	E/W Marriage Certificate	1	Post - 2nd Class or Airmail	19 Oct 2022		£11.00

Year	Qtr	District	Vol	Page	Reg	Ent	NoDOR
1896	Mar	Stoke D	5b	467			

Shipping Method Summary		
Shipping Method	Quantity	Total
Post - 2nd Class or Airmail	1 at £0.00	£0.00
	Shipping Total:	£0.00

Order Total: £11.00

Please note: Mail delivery time should be added to the stated despatch date to calculate when your order should reach you.

ORDERS CAN NOT BE AMENDED OR CANCELLED ONCE THE ORDER HAS BEEN BOOKED. THIS INCLUDES DELIVERY ADDRESS, SHIPPING UPGRADES AND CERTIFICATE INFORMATION. PLEASE ENSURE ALL INFORMATION IS CORRECT BEFORE COMPLETING PURCHASE.

GO BACK   CONFIRM

25. If the details are not correct, then click the blue **Go Back** button to amend the details.
26. Otherwise click the blue **Confirm** button and the **Secure Payment Page** will display.

worldpay from FIS

Help   FAQs   Security

Secure Payment Page
This payment page has been created by WorldPay for GRO Payment. Please review your purchase details, then select a card or payment to proceed to the next page.

Select language   English

GRO Payment
Description   **GRO Basket**
Amount   **£11.00**

Select your payment method

Mastercard   Visa   Maestro

Cancel

worldpay from FIS   For help with your payment visit the: WorldPay from FIS Help.

© 2008 WorldPay Limited

27. Choose how you want to pay.
28. Once you have completed your order, you should be returned to the GRO website.
29. Once you have completed your order, click the **Logout** option on the top right-hand side of the screen.

Chapter 6

Summary

This chapter will describe the history of the census and the content of the census record for each year.

History of the census

A census has been taken every year since 1801. Prior to 1841 the census showed just numbers of people – no names. The country was divided into districts and sub-districts based on the Poor Law. The registration districts were given a unique code number. For example, the 1861 census had a general code of RG 09 followed by the piece number which indicates the area of the country covered by the records. An example would be RG 09/3461. The code HO stands for Home Office and RG for General Register Office.

1801 to 1831
The early censuses 1801-1831 showed the number of inhabited and uninhabited houses, number of families, numbers of men and women, broad occupation categories and baptism, marriage and burial statistics.

1841 census Code HO 107. Census date 6 June 1841
The ages of anyone under fifteen were recorded as given to the enumerator. The ages of people over fifteen were rounded down to nearest five years. So, a forty-three-year-old person was recorded as forty, and a forty-seven-year-old would be recorded as forty-five. It was written in pencil and gave the full names of individuals, their age and sex. It also stated whether people were born in the census county or not. This was shown as Y or N (yes or no).

1851 Code HO 107. Census date 30 March 1851
1861 Code RG 09. Census date 7 April 1861
1871 Code RG 10. Census date 2 April 1871
1881 Code RG 11. Census date 3 April 1881

The census records for the years above provided the full name, sex, occupation and exact age, as given by the head of household, as well as marital status and relationship to head of household. In addition you will find parish and county of birth, and any medical disabilities.

1891 Code RG 12. Census date 5 April 1891
1901 Code RG 13. Census date 31 March 1901

In addition to the information in the previous returns, the employment status is now given but this was recorded as stated by the householder so it may be unreliable.

1911 Code RG 13. Census date 2 April 1911

With each progressive year, more information is noted on the census. In 1911 we find an individual sheet per household with a full address and the number of rooms occupied by the family. In addition each married woman had to give length of marriage, number of children born, number died and number still living. There is also a copy of the enumerator's summary book which may provide more information.

1921 Code RG 15. Census date 19 June 1921

This census was due to be taken in April but was delayed until 19 June 1921 due to the coalminers' Black Friday Strike and the threat of further industrial unrest. The return is an individual schedule for each household and provides the full address of the property, names of the household and their relationship to head of household. Age is given in years and completed months. The sex of each individual is noted as well as the marital status. The title of this column is Marriage or Orphanhood and everyone over fifteen years of age is recorded as single, married, or widowed. If the individual was divorced, D was recorded in this column. For children under fifteen, the presence (or not) of parents was noted; were both parents alive, father dead, mother dead or both dead?

The individual's occupation shows if they were in full or part-time education, the name and type of employer or if they were working on their own account. If the person was out of work, then generally the name of their last employer would be given (if known) and then an added note as out of work. The employer's address was to be given unless they were in private employment. Each married man, widower or widow was required to record the number of children or stepchildren under the age of sixteen in a table on the right-hand side of the sheet. This is an improvement on the 1911 census which required only married women to record the number of children born, alive and dead.

Presently in 2023, the 1921 census records are available on Findmypast website for a fee or free at The National Archives at Kew.

Who distributed the census forms?

Local people were employed as enumerators; their task was to deliver the forms to each household before the census date and to collect them after the census date. An enumerator could help with the form completion if the householder was illiterate.

BUT errors could and did occur! They could mishear or misspell a name, miss a house or not list everyone. Errors could occur in the 1841 to 1901 census records when the information was copied from the forms into the enumerators' books after which the forms were destroyed. These books were pre-printed in a standard format, all having the same page numbers. In order to make the books unique, every other page was stamped with a consecutive FOLIO number. So a full census reference would be RG 09 / 3461 Folio 60 Page 23.

From 1851 the census records of institutions such as hospitals, workhouses, barracks and prisons categorised the individuals as patient or inmate, officer, servant or visitor. There are census records for Royal Navy and merchant ships from 1861. The census of Army units overseas was not taken until 1911, and in 1921 the RAF were included.

The records for the 1911 and 1921 censuses are copies of the forms completed by each householder.

Finding Census Records

The 1881 census is free to view on all commercial websites, such as Findmypast, Ancestry and so on, but you will probably have to register and login with a password. But no payment is required for the 1881 census.

The 1881 census is also available at the Family Search website. You can search the 1881 and other census years on this website but you will only find transcriptions. You need to go to a commercial website, such as Ancestry or Findmypast, to view the actual record and pay a subscription to download an image.

You will find census records on the FreeCen website which is free to use but does not give complete coverage of the country or census images.

Missing Census Records

If you cannot find an ancestor on a census, they may have been missed by the enumerator. But remember, there are some parts of the census records that are either missing or damaged. This article on The National Archives website will help you identify if there are missing records for an area in which your ancestors lived. Type the following into your web browser:

https://blog.nationalarchives.gov.uk/missing-from-the-census

The commercial websites also have details of missing records for each census year.

The 1939 National Register

What happened after 1921? The 1931 records were destroyed in a fire during the Second World War and no census was taken in 1941. Census year records are sealed for one hundred years.

However, on 29 September 1939, a few weeks after war had been declared, a **National Register** was taken to enable the Government to issue identity cards, ration books and identify all those who could be called up for military service. This is a valuable record and will give you details of your ancestors who were alive on that date but have since died. The details of those alive on that day, but potentially still alive today, have been redacted (blacked out).

The actual birth date, occupation and address are given for each individual. However, the actual birth dates might not be correct as some of our ancestors may not have been clear as to their actual date of birth. Changes of address should have been reported under the National Registration Act, which was repealed in 1952, but that rarely happened. After the war, the Register was used as the basis of the National Health Service and changes, particularly married names of women, were made until 1991 when the NHS ceased using the original Register.

This valuable register is available on the Findmypast and Ancestry websites and can be searched without charge but for full details you will need a subscription.

Chapter 7

Summary

This chapter will provide a step-by-step guide as to how to use the Family Search and FreeCEN websites.

So how do you find your ancestors on the census?

We have found that my grandfather George TRICE married Louisa CREBER in 1896 in Devonport, Devon. Hopefully we will find out where both were born. I conducted a search for George in the 1901 census to find his wife and any children.

How to use Family Search to search for census records

1. To access the site type www.familysearch.org into your web browser and the screen below will be displayed.

2. If you have not already done so, you will need to create a free account by clicking the **Create Account** button. Once you have signed in, a new screen will appear part of which is shown below.

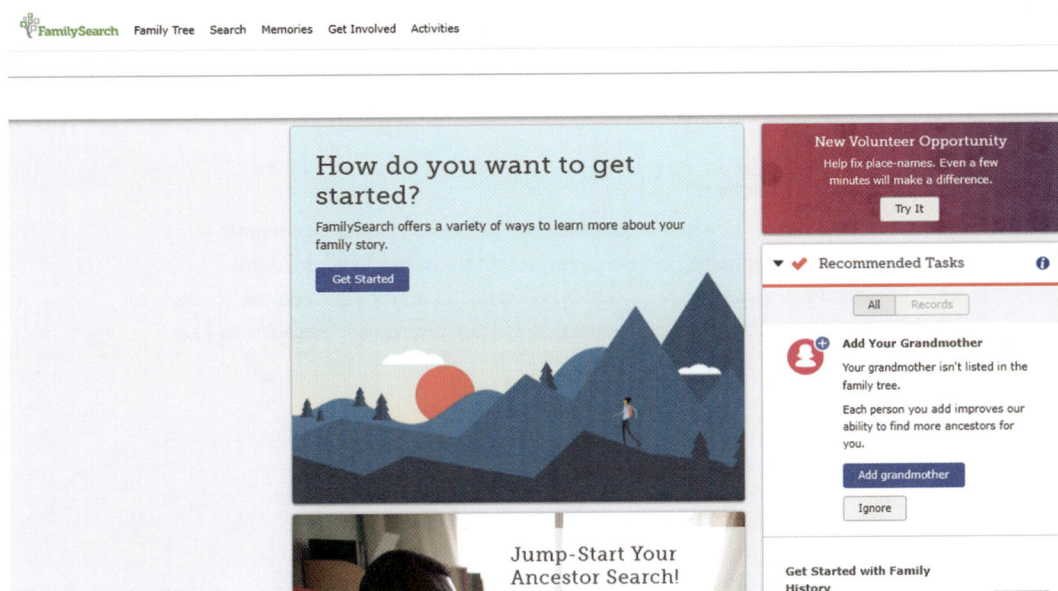

3. Click on **Search** in the menu bar and from the drop-down list and click on **Records.**

4. The next screen has a variety of ways for conducting our research. Let us look at each option in detail.

5. In this section you can enter your ancestor's name with information on place and birth or death year. We will use this option when we look at parish records later.

6. The section labelled **Search by Place** can be useful if you want to restrict your search to a particular place.

7. But we are interested in census records and so go to **Find a Collection.**

8. In the **Collection Title** box, enter **1901 Eng** and you will be offered two collections.

9. Click on the England and Wales Census 1901 option.

Find a Collection

Your ancestor's record belongs to a collection of similar documents— Argentina Baptisms, for example, or United States Census, 1940. Searching a specific collection is one way to narrow your search. If you don't know the collection's exact title, start typing, and we'll try to help you.

Collection Title

1901 Eng

England and Wales Census, 1901

England, Norfolk Non-conformist Records, 1613-1901

10.   The next screen will provide you the opportunity to enter your ancestor's name.

England and Wales Census, 1901

Census returns of England and Wales, 1901.

⊘ HOW TO USE THIS COLLECTION

First Names

Last Names

Place
City, County, State, Province, or Coun

Year
Birth or Death Year

🔍 SEARCH   MORE OPTIONS

11.   Enter George in the **First Names** box, Trice in the **Last Names** box and Devonport, Devon in the **Place** box. You can leave the **Year** box blank.

12.   The next screen will give you some matches to the data you entered. The best matches will be shown at the top of the list.

Filtered Results (33)   ⇄ PREFERENCES   🔍 SEARCH

✓ Collection: Censuses & Lists, England and Wales Census, 1901 (33) ⊗

Collection   Sex   Race   Birth   Residence

Name	Events	Relationships			
George Trice Principal England and Wales Census, 1901	**Census** 31 March 1901 East Stonehouse, Devon, England, United Kingdom **Birth** 1899 Devonport, Devon, England, United Kingdom	**Parents** George Trice, Louisa Trice	👤	⬙	🖹
George Trice Principal England and Wales Census, 1901	**Census** 31 March 1901 East Stonehouse, Devon, England, United Kingdom **Birth** 1871 Brighton, Sussex, England, United Kingdom	**Spouses** Louisa Trice **Children** George Trice	👤	⬙	🖹

13.   At the top of the list is potentially a match to a George TRICE. This is a child born in 1899 with parents George and Louisa TRICE.

14.   The second line shows his parents.

15.   Click on the **document icon** on the right-hand side of the screen for the second record, and you will be shown more details of the family.

George Trice
Census • England and Wales Census, 1901

SAVE   EDIT   SHARE

Name	George Trice
Sex	Male
Age	30
Event Date	31 Mar 1901
Event Place	East Stonehouse, Devon, England, United Kingdom
Event Place (Original)	East Stonehouse, Devonshire, England
Sub-District	East Stonehouse
Registration District	East Stonehouse
Event Type	Census
Birth Year (Estimated)	1871
Birthplace	Brighton, Sussex
Marital Status	Married
Occupation	LANCE SERGEANT R M L I
Relationship to Head of Household	Head
Event Place Note	Durnford Street
Page Number	2
Piece/Folio	140
Schedule Type	17

16. You will see that George was born in Brighton, Sussex. If you scroll down, you will see that his wife's name is Louisa and she was born in Ireland.

17. They have a son, George, born in Devonport now aged two.

18. You also have his father's occupation as a Lance Sergeant in the RMLI.

19. In this census record, the reference is not easy to find. Only the Piece / Folio 140 and Page 2 are given. In fact, the piece number is not given.

20. On the left-hand side of the screen it shows that the image can be found on the Findmypast website.

21. The right-hand side may show that there is a match on someone's family tree on the Family Search and some other census matches.

22. So now we know where George was born and we can go back to the FreeBMD search to identify which year and quarter his birth was registered.

23. This is the image we saw in a previous chapter.

Surname	First name(s)	District	Vol	Page		
Births Sep 1870 (>99%)						
Trice	George William	E. Ashford	2a	665	Info	
Births Mar 1871 (>99%)						
Trice	George	Brighton	2b	260	Info	
Trice	George Frederick	Thanet	2a	814	Info	
Births Jun 1871 (>99%)						
Trice	George Thomas	Portsea	2b	453	Info	
Births Mar 1872 (>99%)						
TRICE	George William	Sheppey	2a	810	Info	
Births Mar 1874 (>99%)						
Trice	George W V	Elham	2A	923	Info	
Births Dec 1876 (>99%)						
TRICE	George	Steyning	2b	278	Info	

24. The only George TRICE born in Brighton is the second entry on the screen.

25. So his birth registration was made in the first quarter of 1871 and the volume is 2b and the page is 260.

26. This means he was either born in late 1870 or early 1871 and therefore we could find him in the 1871, 1881 and 1891 census.

27. On the display we saw on the last screen, there were a couple of other census records for George TRICE.

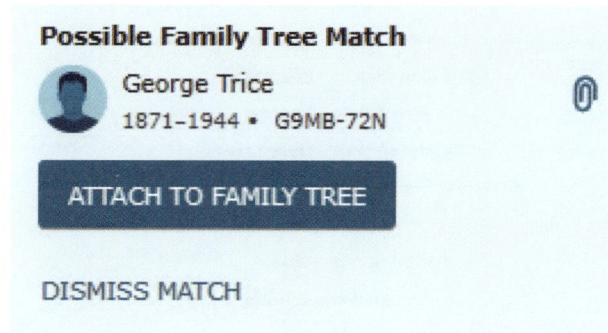

Possible Family Tree Match

George Trice
1871–1944 • G9MB-72N

ATTACH TO FAMILY TREE

DISMISS MATCH

Similar Records

George Trice
England and Wales Census, 1911

George Trice
England and Wales Census, 1881

28. Click on the 1881 link and the right-hand side of the screen displays the record.

George Trice
Census • England and Wales Census, 1881

SAVE   EDIT   SHARE

Name	**George Trice**
Sex	**Male**
Age	**10**
Event Date	**1881**
Event Place	**Brighton, Sussex, England**
Registration District	**Brighton**
Event Type	**Census**
Residence Note	**Over Street**
Birth Year (Estimated)	**1871**
Birthplace	**Brighton, Sussex, England**
Marital Status	**Single**
Occupation	**Scholar**
Relationship to Head of Household	**Son**
Page Number	**8**
Piece/Folio	**1089/27**
Registration Number	**RG11**

29. At the top of the panel, click on blue **View Record** button.

Census • England and Wales Census, 1881

SAVE   EDIT   SHARE

Name	**George Trice**
Sex	**Male**
Age	**10**
Event Date	**1881**
Event Place	**Brighton, Sussex, England**
Registration District	**Brighton**
Event Type	**Census**
Residence Note	**Over Street**
Birth Year (Estimated)	**1871**
Birthplace	**Brighton, Sussex, England**
Marital Status	**Single**
Occupation	**Scholar**
Relationship to Head of Household	**Son**
Page Number	**8**
Piece/Folio	**1089/27**
Registration Number	**RG11**

30.   This clearly shows the reference as follows RG 11 Piece 1089 Folio 27 Page 8.

So what do the images look like?

This is the image for the 1881 census for George TRICE aged ten.

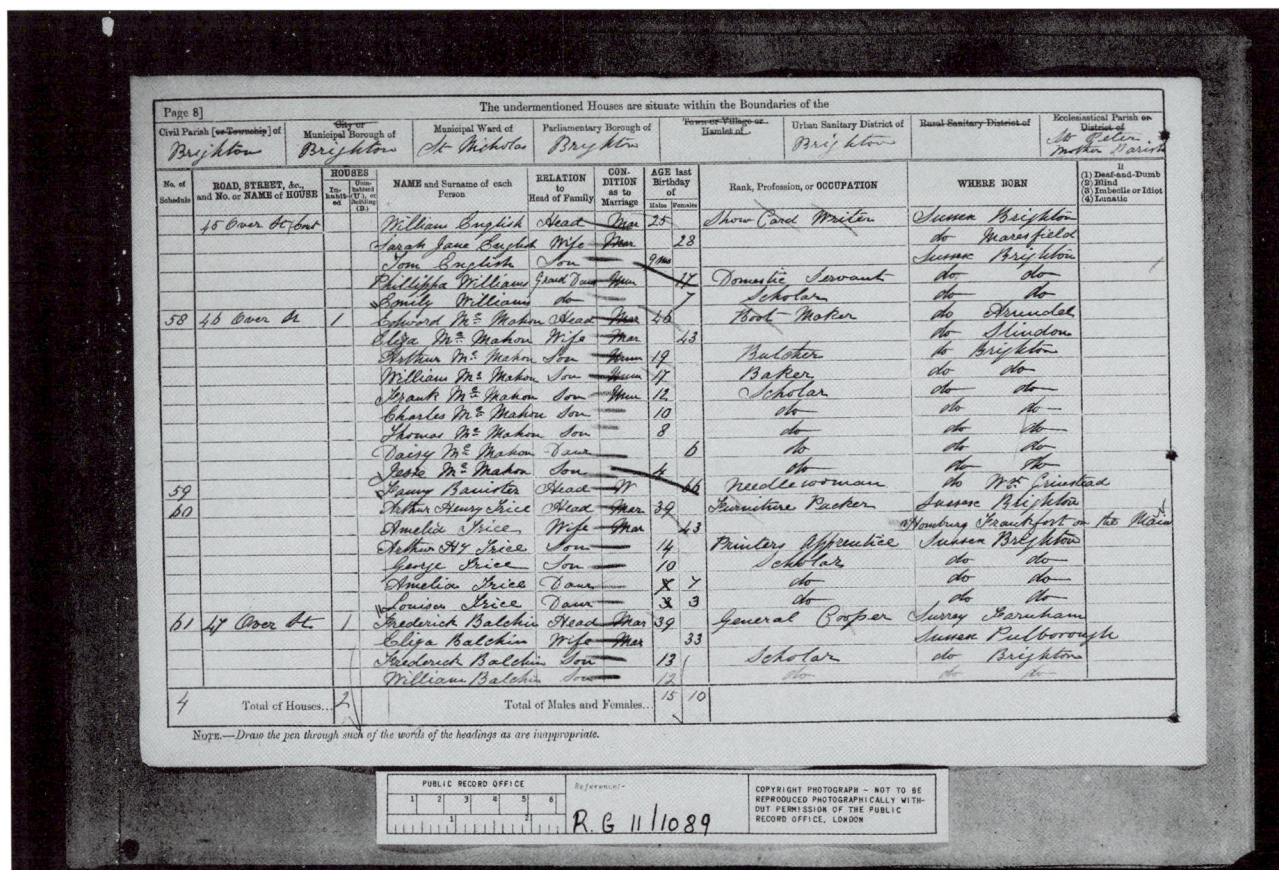

I have magnified the portion that includes the Trice family.

There are three families living in 46 Over Street. They are Edward McMAHON, his wife and seven children, a widow Fanny BANNISTER, and Arthur Henry TRICE, his wife and three children. The 1881 census does not tell us how many rooms the TRICE family occupied in a house with three separate households.

How do we know there are three households? There are two indicators and the first is how many heads of household are there for each address. In addition there is a single mark \ at the left-hand side of a name indicating the end of each household and a double mark \\ at the end of each physical house. The other marks are made by the civil servants as they counted the different statistical data. Sometimes these marks go through the information we are interested in such as ages.

The 1911 and 1921 censuses provide an individual schedule for each household so there could be more than one schedule for 46 Over Street in the 1911 census, especially if multiple families still live in the house. On a commercial website, you can search an address and see who else lives in the house.

How to use FreeCEN to search census records

This is a free website but does not cover all the areas of UK or all of the census years. It relies upon volunteers who transcribe the areas and years they choose. You will not find George TRICE on this website. But I will demonstrate how to use the site using another of my ancestors.

1. Enter www.freecen.org.uk into your web browser and this will be displayed.

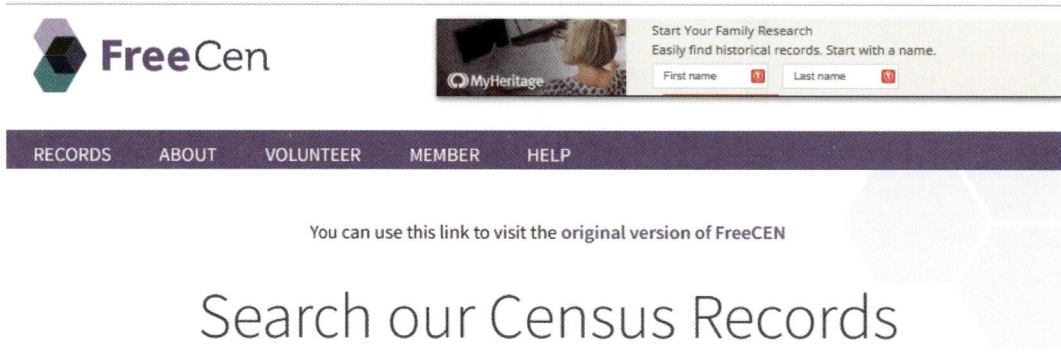

2. Click on **Records** in the menu bar to find out which counties are covered in each census year.
3. On the next screen you can select a county in this box.

4. I selected Devon from the drop-down list and clicked the **View County Records** button.
5. This is part of the next screen.

Database Records for Devon as of 16 Oct 2022

Back to Totals for All Counties

---Places in Devon---

You may view the Database Records for a specific Place and if there are Pieces Online also get a list of Names currently in the Database.
Note: Brackets after the Place name indicate there are Pieces Online for those years.

Place ⓘ

Select a Place in Devon …

View Place Records

Totals for All Places in Devon

Where applicable you can use the Action buttons to view a list of Pieces (including Civil Parish names)

Note: A * next to the number of Pieces Online indicates that only part of one or more pieces is currently online - use View Pieces to see details

Year	Pieces Online	Total Pieces	% Online	Records Online	New Pieces Online	Actions
1841	77	78	98.7	531721	0	View Pieces
1851	72	94	76.6	440743	3	View Pieces

6. If you wish, you can select a place to find if your area is covered. The table on the right-hand side shows you the percentage of records available online for each census year.
7. Click on **Search** on the menu bar at the top of the screen to start a search.
8. Go back to step one to see the website search screen to enter your ancestor's details.
9. I entered CREBER, Samuel, birth date range 1795 to 1797 and selected Devon from the county drop-down list. This is my two times great-grandfather.
10. Scroll down and click the **Search** button.

Revise Search | New Search | About This Query | Printable Format

When you searched for:

First Name	Last Name	Exact Match?	Birth Year	Census Year
SAMUEL	CREBER	Yes	1795 - 1797	All

Birth County
Devon

We found 1 Result

Listed by date. Select a heading to sort by that column; select again to reverse the order. See individual details by selecting the View button.

Detail	Individual	Birth County	Birth Place	Birth	Census	Census County	Census Place
View 1	Samuel CREBER	Devon	Stoke Damerel	1797	1851	Devon	Stonehouse

Advertisement

We found records about Samuel CREBER

11. Across the top you will see buttons that allow you to **Revise Search** or to start a **New Search**.
12. One result is found and the record can be viewed by clicking the **View 1** button.

Previous Dwelling   Next Dwelling   Printable Format

Census	County	District	Civil Parish	Ecclesiastical Parish	Piece	Enumeration District	Folio	Page	Schedule	House Number	House or Street Name
1851	Devon (DEV)	East Stonehouse	East Stonehouse	East Stonehouse	1880	1a	23	39	132	2	Cremell Point

13. This part of the screen shows the place, house number and house or street name.
14. The census reference is HO 107 [for the 1851 census] piece number 1880, folio 23 and page 39.
15. There are buttons across the top that allow you to see the record for the dwelling either side of the chosen dwelling.
16. Scroll down for the next part of the screen which is shown below.

New Search   Revise Search   Back to Results   Generate Citation

Surname	Forenames	Relationship	Marital Status	Sex	Age	Occupation	Birth County	Birth Place	Disability	Notes
CREBER	Samuel	Head	M	M	54	Sawler Dock	Devon	Stoke Damerel		Superannuated
CREBER	Elizabeth	Wife	M	F	55		Devon	Dartmouth		
CREBER	James	Son	-	M	12	Scholar	Devon	Devonport		
SCOTT	Mary	Dau	M	F	23		Devon	Devonport		
SCOTT	Elizabeth	Grndau	-	F	2		Devon	Stonehouse		

17. This shows you the family in the chosen dwelling place. Across the top are buttons to start a new search or to revise the search.

Summary

So we have found George TRICE's birth registration, the registration of his marriage to Louisa CREBER and records of George in the 1901 and 1881 census - all good evidence. I have found out from the 1881 census that his father was Arthur Henry TRICE who was married to a German lady, Amelie. They had another son Arthur Hy aged fourteen and two daughters aged seven and three.

Arthur Henry was born in Brighton around 1842 so I could look for his birth registration and find him in the 1851, 1861 and 1871 census records. In the 1851 census Arthur is nine and has a twin brother Frederick. Their father is George TRICE aged thirty-two and born in Sheerness Kent and his wife is Jane aged thirty-two and born in Leominster, Herefordshire. George is born around 1820 which takes us to Parish Registers.

The next step is to trace my grandfather through all the census records from 1881 including the 1939 Register.

Exercise 5

Practice in using the Family Search website

Remember… less is more! In census searches always use birth date range as one year plus or minus a year.

1. **Charles Darwin was born on 12 Feb 1809 in Shrewsbury, England. He became an English naturalist who was famous for his theory of natural selection. He died in about 1882.**

   Find his **address** in the 1881 census.
   Address………………………………………………………………

2. **John James Sainsbury was born on 12 Jun 1844 at 5 Oakley Street, Lambeth. His first job was with a grocer in the New Cut, Lambeth. After gaining experience with several other grocery businesses, he went on to found the Sainsbury's supermarket chain.**

   Find his **address** in the 1881 census.
   Address………………………………………………………………

3. **Thomas Hardy, the British author, was born in 1840 in a hamlet called Higher Brockhampton in Dorset, three miles from the town of Dorchester.**

   Find his **address** in the 1881 census.
   Address……………………………………………………………….

4. **William Gilbert Grace (18 Jul 1848–23 Oct 1915) was an English cricketer who was born in Gloucestershire and was a doctor by profession.**

   Find his **address** in the 1881 census.
   Address………………………………………………………………

5. **Emmeline Pankhurst (1858 - 1928), better known as Emily Pankhurst, founded the Women's Social and Political Union and worked throughout her life for the cause of women's suffrage. In 1879 she married Richard Marsden Pankhurst.**

   Find her **address** in the 1881 census.
   Address………………………………………………………………

6. **Sir Winston Leoard Spencer Churchill, KG, OM, CH, TD, FRS, PC (30 Nov 1874 – 24 Jan 1965) was a British politician and best known as Prime Minister of the United Kingdom during the Second World War.**

   Find his **address** in the 1881 census.
   Address………………………………………………………………

Exercise 6
Practice in using the FreeCEN website

1. **Thomas Hoar was born in Portsmouth in about 1828 and he was a coastguard.**

   Find his address in the **1861 census.**
   Address...
   Census reference..

2. **John H Cross was born in Portsmouth in about 1813.**

   Find his address in the **1891 census.**
   Address...
   Census reference..

3. **Joseph W Page was born in Portsmouth in about 1861.**

   Find his address in the **1891 census.**
   Address...
   Census reference..

Chapter 8

Summary

The evidence of life events before 1837 can be found in a variety of parish records. The most common records are the parish registers which record baptisms, marriage and burials. This chapter describes the history of these registers.

The History of Parish Registers

Parish registers record baptisms, marriages and burials - just one item in many other parish records. Prior to the establishment of the Church of England, parish incumbents were required to store important records, accounts and the church silver securely. This was done by placing these precious items in what was called the **parish chest**. You can read more about the parish chests typing this link into your web browser.

www.familysearch.org/en/wiki/introduction_to_English_Poor_Law_and_Parish_Chest_Records_ (National_Institute)

Thomas Cromwell, English lawyer and statesman, held many roles and offices when serving his king, and on 5 September 1538 he was created Vicar General to Henry VIII. This gave him executive powers to organise the church. He demanded in the name of the king that each parish was to keep a register as a means of determining inheritance rights – but some people saw it as a prelude to the imposition of taxes!

In 1597 Elizabeth I ordered the use of a parchment book to ensure the records would withstand any damage from insects and damp. All the old paper records were to be copied into the new book and kept in the Parish chest.

In 1598 annual copies of the parish records were to be sent to the bishop and these are known as Bishops' Transcripts. A copy of previous year's entries was to be sent within one month of Easter. This practice ended in late nineteenth century.

These life events – baptisms, marriages and burials - were recorded in a plain book, and as a result the entries are not always in straight lines. Sometimes a baptism, marriage or burial is not recorded on the actual date of the event and could be added later in the register with a note on the page where it should have been entered.

The Commonwealth period 1649-1660 removed control of life events from the established church. You may struggle to find records, particularly for marriages, in this period.

There is a history of parish registers in England online. You can read more by typing this url into your browser:

www.familysearch.org/en/wiki/History_of_Parish_Registers_in_England

So what will I find in the parish registers?

Many of the early records have probably been lost or damaged, but it is still worth searching the parish register records. Those that you do find are not as detailed as the records post-1837 or the census returns. You will often find a baptism which states *John son of John Smith and his wife*. A burial record might just be *John Smith buried on 9 July 1722*. No idea of age or to whom they might be related.

Baptisms did not necessarily take place close to the date of birth; you may find two or more children in the same family being baptised on the same day. This is not an indication of a multiple birth but could be a family having a newborn and an older child baptised at the same time.

If there is an age given in a burial record, it might not be accurate. You might come across a note that the burial was *in wool*. This practice was introduced by an Act in Parliament in 1666 to support the woollen trade. By 1678 a fine of £5 was imposed for any failure to bury someone in wool. It was a requirement that an affidavit be sworn in front of a Justice of the Peace confirming burial in wool, with the punishment of a £5 fee for noncompliance. This remained in force until 1814 but was generally ignored after 1770.

Marriages

Regardless of religious belief, marriages had to be conducted before an Anglican clergyman. Prior to 1754, Canon law required banns to be called or a licence to be issued for a marriage to take place. Couples who tried to avoid a marriage requiring the calling of banns or a licence either eloped to Gretna Green in Scotland or sought a priest who was not controlled by the Church. Such priests were to be found in Fleet Prison in London.

The 1754 Hardwicke's Clandestine Marriages Act required marriages to be in an Anglican church. Exceptions were made for Quakers and Jews. The Act suggested optional printed marriage and banns registers. In 1812, Sir George Rose's Parochial Registers Act saw the introduction of printed baptism and burial registers.

If you would like to know more about the law and marriage, I can recommend the book by Rebecca Probert entitled *Marriage Law for Genealogists* published by Takeaway.

Gregorian Calendar

If you see the year **1752** for an event in a parish register – **beware!!**
It's all to do with the change from the Julian calendar to the Gregorian calendar.

The **Julian calendar** was introduced by Julius Caesar in 45BC. This was used for centuries but eventually there had to be a change. The Julian calendar assumed that the time between vernal equinoxes is 365.25 days, when in fact it is presently almost eleven minutes shorter. This error meant that time accumulated at the rate of about three days every four centuries. This resulted in the equinox occurring on 11 March, an error of about ten days. An answer had to be found to correct these extra days.

The **Gregorian calendar** was introduced by Pope Gregory XIII on 24 February 1582. Britain and the British Empire adopted the Gregorian calendar in 1752 - this was 170 years *after* Catholic Europe had made the change by which time it was necessary to correct the calendar by eleven days. The result was...

Wednesday, 2 September 1752 was followed by Thursday, 14 September 1752!!

Prior to 1752 the start of the year was 25 March or Lady Day. So you will see entries *before* 1752 as 1 January to 24 March. The 24 March was the last day of the year, making 25 March the start of the new year. For example, a baptism on 1 March 1667 could be followed by a baptism in the *following* month recorded as 19 April 1668.

You will see this clearly in parish registers before 1752 where the year changes after 24 March.

So in registers before 1752 do check the year of the event! You may see dates given as Old Style (Julian) and New Style (Gregorian). I have seen gravestones with the date shown as $170\frac{1}{2}$ meaning 1701 (Old Style) or 1702 (New Style).

Incidentally, Lady Day was the day when new contracts were agreed between landowners and tenant farmers. If you add eleven days to 25 March, you come to 5 April which was adjusted to 6 April which is the start of a new tax year in the UK!

Where can I find parish register records?

On the Family Search website you will only see names and dates but if you are lucky, there might be a link to further information. Commercial websites like Findmypast and Ancestry have indexed register records for some counties. FreeREG is another free website but the number of records is limited as it depends on the number of volunteers available.

You will have to actually see the original parish records to get the full details and these are held at the relevant county record offices. Many family history societies have produced transcriptions of local parish records in their areas, so check their websites for details too.

Points to note when searching

- always use **SURNAME** variations
- add **county or parish** to reduce the number of records
- add **date range** for the same reason
- `use **wildcards** in your searches. For example...

  Tri* - *all names beginning with Tri*
  Tri?? - *all names with two characters after Tri*

- view original registers – not all indexes have complete information
- use other family members – mother, father, siblings – to validate your selection or use as an alternative search term.

Chapter 9

Summary

This chapter will take you through a step-by-step guide to finding parish records on Family Search and FreeReg websites.

How to find parish register records in Family Search

Unfortunately, although I have found George TRICE's father Arthur Henry TRICE, I have not been able to trace his father in the parish registers.

So I will use another ancestor, my great-grandfather James George Hall CREBER who was born in 1839. I discovered from the census records that his father was Samuel CREBER born in 1797. We are going to use the Family Search website that we used for the census records.

Family Search is always adding records so some of the following screens may show other records as well as the records of the individuals I have indicated.

To start, log on to gain access to the website as you did in chapter seven. You should then be at the page that has this section.

First Names

Last Names

Place

City, County, State, Province, or Cour

Year

Birth or Death Year

🔍 SEARCH   MORE OPTIONS

1. I entered Samuel in the **First Names** box and CREBER in the **Last Names** box. In the **Place** box I typed in Devon and the **Year box** 1797.
2. Then I clicked on **More Options** so I can enter some more information to display the extended box.

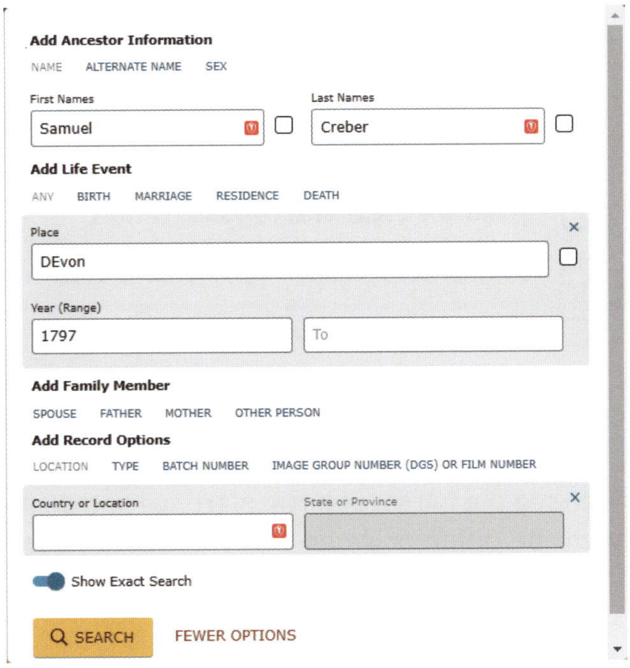

3. I can now add to the year by entering an end date, 1837, in the **To** box. I could add more information if I had the data.
4. Click the **Search** button and the screen that is displayed is shown here.

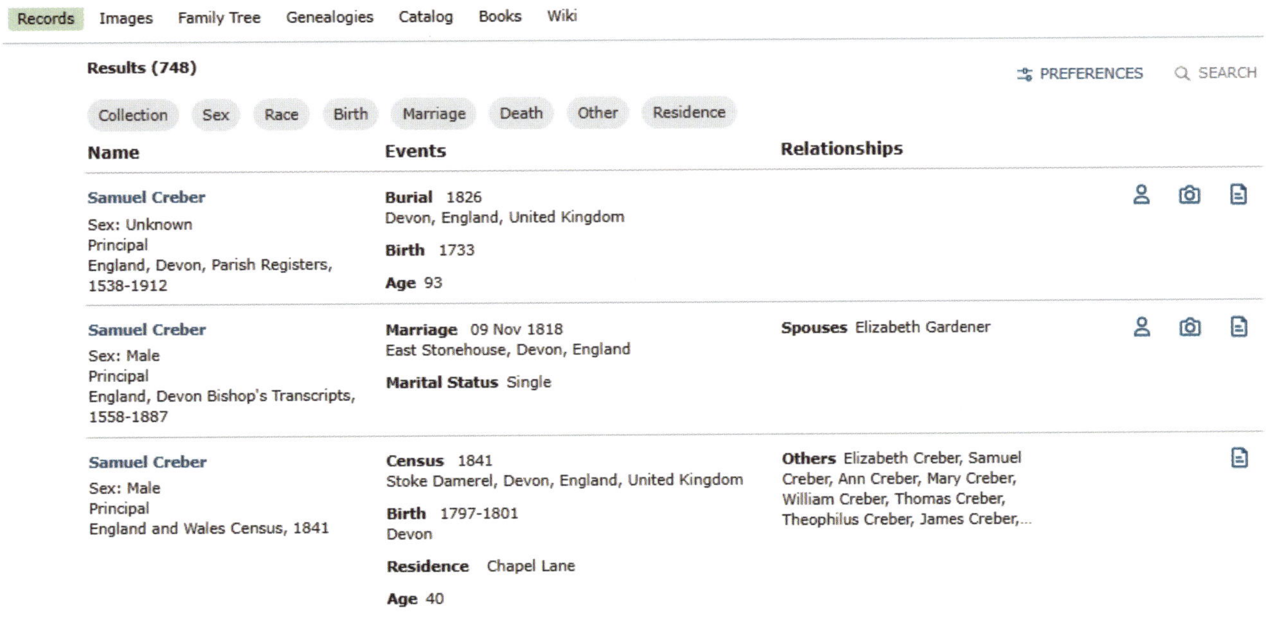

5. This is a mixture of baptism, marriage, burial and census records.
6. Initially, I want the baptism record for Samuel. At the top of the screen are some grey buttons as shown here.

7. Click on the **Collection** button so we can eliminate some of the entries. The list of available databases is displayed on the right-hand side of the screen.

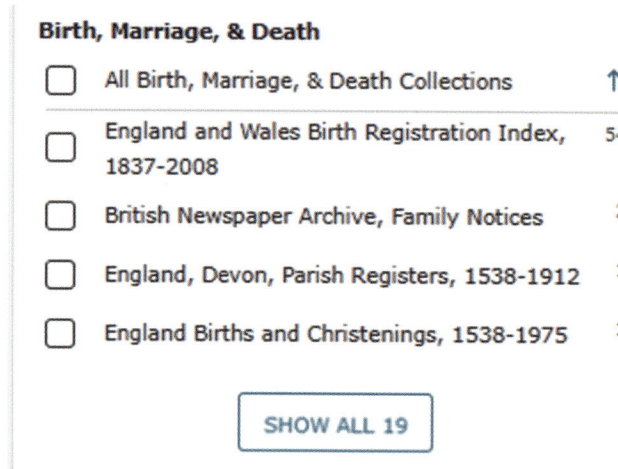

Birth, Marriage, & Death

- ☐ All Birth, Marriage, & Death Collections ⇅
- ☐ England and Wales Birth Registration Index, 1837-2008 — 54
- ☐ British Newspaper Archive, Family Notices — 2
- ☐ England, Devon, Parish Registers, 1538-1912 — 1
- ☐ England Births and Christenings, 1538-1975 — 1

SHOW ALL 19

8. Click first **Show All** to see the full list of birth, marriage and death collections. (The number after **Show All** might be different when you try this as other records might have been added.) Select those records that should reveal a christening or baptism by ticking the relevant boxes as shown below.

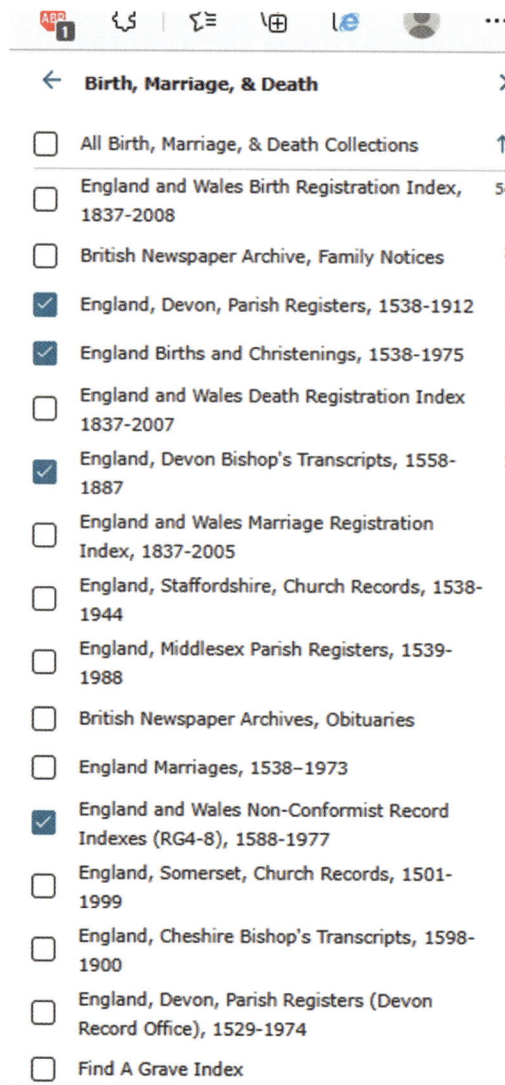

← **Birth, Marriage, & Death** ›

- ☐ All Birth, Marriage, & Death Collections ↑
- ☐ England and Wales Birth Registration Index, 1837-2008 — 54
- ☐ British Newspaper Archive, Family Notices — 2
- ☑ England, Devon, Parish Registers, 1538-1912 — 1
- ☑ England Births and Christenings, 1538-1975 — 1
- ☐ England and Wales Death Registration Index 1837-2007 — 1
- ☑ England, Devon Bishop's Transcripts, 1558-1887 — 1
- ☐ England and Wales Marriage Registration Index, 1837-2005
- ☐ England, Staffordshire, Church Records, 1538-1944
- ☐ England, Middlesex Parish Registers, 1539-1988
- ☐ British Newspaper Archives, Obituaries
- ☐ England Marriages, 1538–1973
- ☑ England and Wales Non-Conformist Record Indexes (RG4-8), 1588-1977
- ☐ England, Somerset, Church Records, 1501-1999
- ☐ England, Cheshire Bishop's Transcripts, 1598-1900
- ☐ England, Devon, Parish Registers (Devon Record Office), 1529-1974
- ☐ Find A Grave Index

9. At the foot of the list is the **Apply Application Filter** button. Click it and the main display changes to show these records.

Filtered Results (47)

✓ Collection: Birth, Marriage, & Death, England Births and Christenings, 1538-1975 (17) ✕

✓ Collection: Birth, Marriage, & Death, England and Wales Non-Conformist Record Indexes (RG4-8), 1588-1977 (2) ✕

✓ Collection: Birth, Marriage, & Death, England, Devon Bishop's Transcripts, 1558-1887 (10) ✕

⇌ PREFERENCES   🔍 SEARCH

SHOW MORE

Collection | Sex | Race | Birth | Marriage | Death | Other

Name	Events	Relationships			
Samuel Creber Principal England, Devon, Parish Registers, 1538-1912	**Burial** 1826 Devon, England, United Kingdom **Birth** 1733		👤	📷	📄
Samuel Creber Principal England, Devon Bishop's Transcripts, 1558-1887	**Marriage** 9 November 1818 East Stonehouse, Devon, England	**Spouses** Elizabeth Gardener	👤	📷	📄
Samuel Creber Principal England, Devon, Parish Registers, 1538-1912	**Baptism** 1810 Devon, England, United Kingdom			📷	📄

10.   I can reduce the choices by clicking on the **Birth** button and this box is displayed.

> BIRTHPLACE   BIRTH YEAR (RANGE)
>
> United Kingdom and Ireland (18)
>
> CANCEL   **APPLY**

11.   Click on the **Birth Year** tab to show this box.

> BIRTHPLACE   BIRTH YEA >
>
> 1700 (12)   1800 (11)
>
> CANCEL   **APPLY**

12.   Click on the **1700 (12)** button to show these choices.

> BIRTHPLACE   BIRTH YEAR (RANGE)
>
> **Selected Filter**
> ✓ 1700 (12) ✕
>
> **Browse in 1700**
>
> 1700 (1)   1710 (1)   1730 (4)   1750 (3)   1760 (1)   1790 (2)
>
> CANCEL   **APPLY**

13. There are only two records for 1790 so click on that option and then the **Apply** button.
14. We then have a couple of records to view.

15. Click on the icon on the right-hand side of the screen that looks like a document. This is a section of the screen you will see.

Name	**Samuel Creber**
Sex	**Male**
Christening Date	**19 Mar 1797**
Christening Place	**Stoke Damerel, Devon, England**
Father's Name	**Richard Creber**
Father's Sex	**Male**
Mother's Name	**Elizabeth**
Mother's Sex	**Female**
Event Type	**Christening**

Samuel Creber's Parents and Siblings   OPEN ALL

Richard Creber	Father	M	⌄
Elizabeth	Mother	F	⌄

16. So we have a christening/baptism date and place together with the names of Samuel's father and mother.
17. On the right-hand side you will see other suggested records including census entries which may or may not be related to the person in the main display.

Attached in Family Tree to

Samuel Creber
1797–1855 • LCTP-XVT

Similar Records

Samuel Creber
England and Wales Census, 1851

Samuel Creber
England and Wales Census, 1841

Samuel Creber
England, Devon, Parish Registers, 1538-1912

Samuel Creber
England, Devon Bishop's Transcripts, 1558-1887

Attached To:

Samuel Creber
1797–1855 • LCTP-XVT

At first, it seems Family Search is a bit complicated to use, but there are a lot of records so it's well worth a visit. However, there is a useful guide as to how to use this site more effectively. It can be found by entering the following into your web browser:
www.familysearch.org/en/blog/search-historical-records-update

It is worth persevering with the free online Family Search website - otherwise you will have to visit the appropriate County Record Office to view the parish registers.

How to find parish registers on FreeREG

FreeREG website is very similar to the FreeCEN website we looked at in chapter seven.

1.   Enter www.freereg.org.uk into your web browser and this will be displayed.

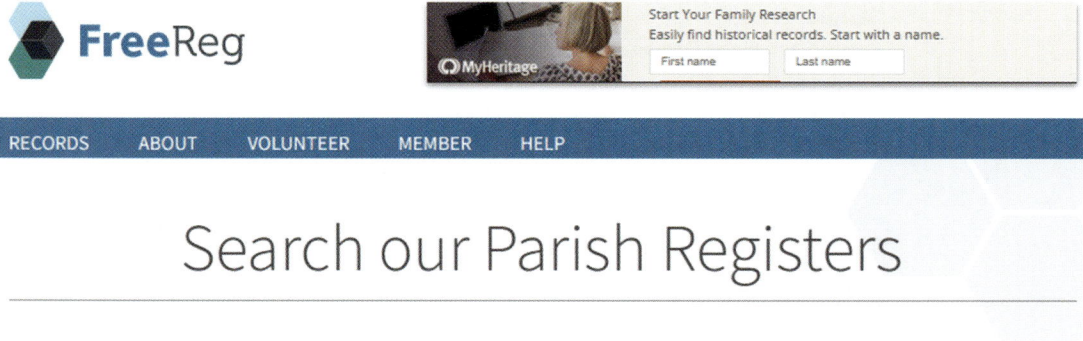

2.   You can click on **Records** in the menu bar to find out which counties and parishes are covered before you start searching. If your parish is not covered then there is no point in searching.
3.   We know George TRICE was born in Sussex so let us check.
4.   This is a portion of the screen you will see. The counties are listed here and I have scrolled down to find Sussex.

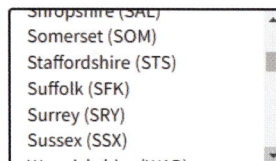

5. Highlight the county name by clicking on it and then click the **Select** button below the table.
6. You will then see a list of places. Scroll down to find Brighton.

Choose a Specific Place

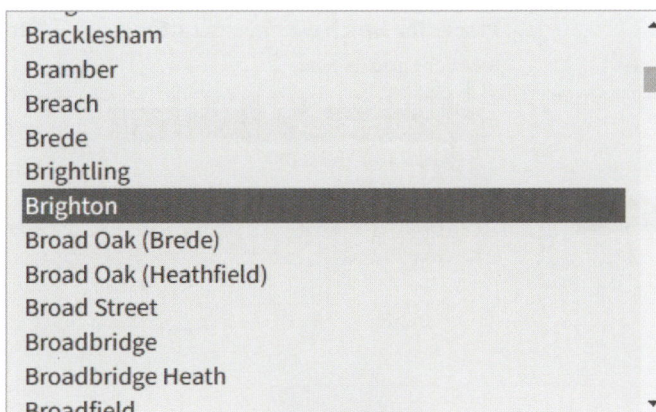

Bracklesham
Bramber
Breach
Brede
Brightling
Brighton
Broad Oak (Brede)
Broad Oak (Heathfield)
Broad Street
Broadbridge
Broadbridge Heath
Broadfield

Select

7. Highlight the place and click the **Select** button in the menu bar. A list of churches within Brighton is shown.

Place	Churches	Registers	Changed	Records	First	Last
Brighton	Chapel Royal	Parish Register	13 Aug 2021	3,329	1823	1881
Brighton	Holy Trinity	Parish Register	05 Nov 2020	152	1871	1881
Brighton	St John the Evangelist	Parish Register	21 Jan 2020	3,074	1846	1881
Brighton	St Margaret	Parish Register	06 Dec 2020	258	1870	1881
Brighton	St Nicholas of Myra	Parish Register	29 Sep 2021	161,707	1559	1891
Brighton	St Peter	Parish Register	08 May 2020	13,316	1840	1873

8. Go to the top of the screen and click on **Search** in the menu bar.
9. On the next screen, enter your ancestor's surname and forename and a range of dates.
10. Select a county and a place, and finally select a baptism, marriage or burial record or all three.
11. I have entered Arthur TRICE, my great-grandfather and the dates 1841 to 1881.
12. I selected Sussex as the county and Brighton as the place as shown on the next page.

Search fields

Surname 🛈	Forename(s) 🛈	First year 🛈	Last year 🛈
Trice	Arthur	1841	1881

County 🛈
Select one to three (hold Ctrl for multiple)

| Staffordshire (STS) |
| Suffolk (SFK) |
| Surrey (SRY) |
| **Sussex (SSX)** |
| Warwickshire (WAR) |

Places for which we have data 🛈
Select one place or none

| **Brighton (Sussex)** |
| Broadwater (Sussex) |
| Burgess Hill (Sussex) |
| Burpham (Sussex) |
| Burton (Sussex) |

Record type

◉ All three types
○ Baptism
○ Marriage
○ Burial

Search options

☐ **Family members** 🛈   ☐ **Witnesses** 🛈   ☐ **Name Soundex** 🛈
☐ **Nearby places** 🛈

[Search]

13. Click **Search** button and four matching records appear.

When you searched for:

First Name	Last Name	Exact Match?	Start Year	End Year	Record Type
ARTHUR	**TRICE**	**Yes**	**1841**	**1881**	**All**

County	Place
Sussex	**Brighton**

Details	Person or persons	Record type	Event date	County	Place : Church : Register type
View 1	Arthur Henry TRICE	Baptism	27 Mar 1842	Sussex	Brighton : St Nicholas of Myra : Parish Register
View 2	Amelie Louise SCHRAMM Arthur Henry TRICE	Marriage	24 Aug 1863	Sussex	Brighton : St Nicholas of Myra : Parish Register
View 3	Frederick Arthur Schramm TRICE	Baptism	11 Jun 1865	Sussex	Brighton : St Nicholas of Myra : Parish Register
View 4	Arthur Henry TRICE	Baptism	01 Aug 1869	Sussex	Brighton : St Nicholas of Myra : Parish Register

14. To see the detail of each record click one of the blue **View** buttons.

Field (only fields with a value are shown)	Value
County	Sussex
Place (Links to more information)	Brighton
Church name (Links to more information)	St Nicholas of Myra
Register type (Links to more information)	Parish Register
Register entry number	2007
Baptism date	27 Mar 1842
Person forename	Arthur Henry
Person sex	M
Father forename	George
Mother forename	Jane
Father surname	TRICE
Person abode	Castle St.
Father occupation	Servant
Transcribed by	Jennifer Litton
File line number	454

Report an Error in this Data

15. This gives me the baptism date for Arthur, the church in which he was baptised and the names of his parents.
16. At the top of the screen are various blue buttons with the name of their function.

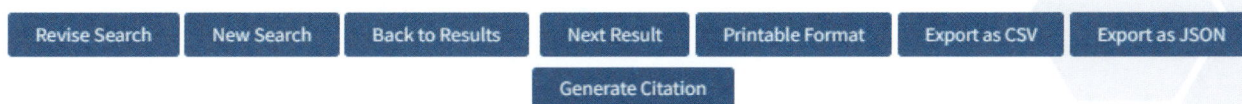

Revise Search   New Search   Back to Results   Next Result   Printable Format   Export as CSV   Export as JSON

Generate Citation

What this also shows is that even after civil registration in 1837, parish registers were still maintained. So it is worthwhile checking these records if available as they could reveal more information to support your research.

Summary of progress

I have found my grandfather's and great-grandfather's birth details and some census entries for both ancestors providing me with the names of their wives and children. The next step is to find out as much as you can about these ancestors and continue tracking them and their parents.

Exercise 7

1. **Charles Darwin was born on 12 Feb 1809 in Shropshire, England. He became an English naturalist who was famous for his theory of *natural selection*. He died in about 1882.**

    Find his **birth /baptism** details.

    Name at baptism...

    Date baptised ....   Date born ....

    Church / parish.................................... Parents...................................

2. **Sir Robert Peel (1788 - 1850) was born in Bury, Lancashire. He was Prime Minister twice, 1834-5 and 1841-6 and one of the greatest Prime Ministers of the nineteenth century. He created the modern police force, unarmed and in blue to be as unlike the army as possible.**

    Find his **birth / baptism** details.

    Name at baptism...

    Date baptised ....   Date born ....

    Church / parish.................................... Parents...................................

3. **Isambard Kingdom Brunel, (1806 –1859) was a British engineer born in Hampshire. Voted the second greatest Briton of all time in a 2002 BBC poll.**

    Find his **birth / baptism** details.

    Name at baptism...

    Date baptised ....   Date born ....

    Church / parish.................................... Parents...................................

Exercise 7

4. **Sir Isaac Newton, PRS, (1643 -1727) was an English physicist, mathematician, astronomer, alchemist, inventor, and natural philosopher who is generally regarded as one of the most influential scientists in history.**

   Find his **birth / baptism** details.

   Name at baptism..

   Date baptised......................... Date born ....

   Church / parish... Parents...

5. **Jane Austen (1775 – 1817) was an English novelist born in Hampshire. She is best known for her six main novels including *Pride and Prejudice.***

   Find her **baptism** details.

   Name at baptism..

   Date baptised ....

   Church / parish... Parents...

Chapter 10

Summary

This chapter provides information on three useful websites for further research. It will also cover finding an ancestor who served in World War One or in the Royal Navy.

Asking questions

Hopefully, you have become familiar with the websites described in the previous chapters. By now you should have started to build your own family tree and I expect the information you have found will have raised some questions. *Where did great-grandfather fight in the First World War*, or more simply, *where can I find out more information about an uncle's occupation*? The census records might have shown that some of your ancestors were scholars; *what does this mean* or *where did they go to school*? On a wider theme you may be thinking what life was like living in a time before the NHS. *Did world events have an impact on my ancestors' lives* is another common question.

You are now starting to think laterally and trying to put some flesh on the bones of your ancestors. In this chapter and the next, I will show you some websites where you can find the answers to some of these questions.

Google

We often use Google to find answers to everyday questions and we can do the same for our family history questions. (Have you ever "Googled" your own name? If not give it a try!).

However, there are some websites that provide a more focussed source of information, and I am going to describe three of these in more detail - **GENUKI, Cyndi's List** and **The National Archives.**

GENUKI

GENUKI is a useful source of links to various archives or websites of interest to family historians. As the name implies, it covers UK and Ireland only.

Type www.genuki.org.uk into your web browser. The website page is shown on the next page.

It looks complicated at first glance but there is a useful guide for first-time users shown below. Click on the button on the right-hand side of the screen labelled **Getting started in genealogy** for detailed help on how to use the website. This is the screen you will see.

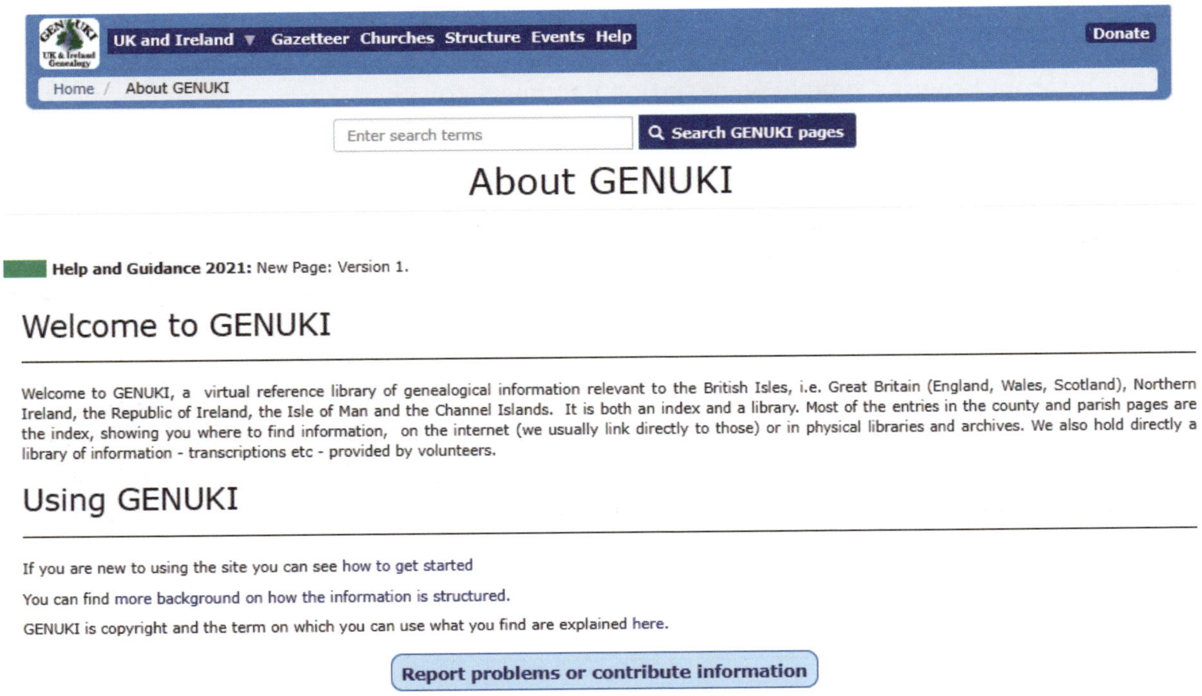

Cyndi's List

Cyndi's list is similar to GENUKI in that it provides links for researchers, but it is American-based and covers worldwide sources of information on the Internet.

This is the website address to type into your browser: www.cyndislist.com.

The home screen is shown on the next page.

HOME   CATEGORIES   WHAT'S NEW   SHOP   SUPPORT US

Cyndi's List

A comprehensive, categorized & cross-referenced list of links that point you to genealogical research sites online.

Your genealogy starting point for more than 25 years!

Ira & Clara Johnson

Categories

Follow Us

Cyndi's List Blog

Mailing List

Browse New Links

Submit a New Link

Report a Broken Link

Welcome to Cyndi's List

Cyndi's List has been a trusted genealogy research site for more than 25 years. *Cyndi's List* is free for everyone to use and it is meant to be your starting point when researching online.

- What exactly is *Cyndi's List*?
  - A categorized & cross-referenced index to genealogical resources on the Internet.
  - A list of links that point you to genealogical research sites online.
  - A **free** jumping-off point for you to use in your online research.
  - A "card catalog" to the genealogical collection in the immense library that is the Internet.
  - Your genealogical research portal onto the Internet.

Donate

Why Donate to Cyndi's List?

Genealogy News Feeds

Louisiana Pre-Adoption Birth Certificates
22/07/2022
Adopted persons age 24 and over who were born in Louisiana may request a non-certified copy of their....

The Genealogy Guys Podcast #406
20/07/2022
New You Can Use and Share! The Guys want to thank everyone in the genealogical community for suppo....

Introducing Historic Native

The National Archives

What is The National Archives? This important organisation is the official archive and publisher of official and Government documents.

Using your Internet browser, type in www.nationalarchives.gov.uk.

This is part of the web page that will be displayed.

THE NATIONAL ARCHIVES   Menu   Search our website

Explore
1,000 years of history

Help with your research   Search the catalogue   Find online collections

There are three buttons to help you:
- **Help with your research**
- **Search the catalogue**
- **Find online collections**

Let us examine each of these options.

Help with your research

Click on this button and below is part of the web page that will be displayed. The most common research guides are shown and more are available if you click the **Use our A – Z index** button just above the gallery of pictures.

Search the catalogue

Go back to the website's home screen and click on the **Search the catalogue** button to access this screen.

One of the features of this part of the website is that you can search all archives, not just those held by the National Archives. This **Explore the catalogue** box allows you to enter your search criteria and to choose **All archives, Other archives only** or **The National Archives** in the **Held by** box.

Use the **Explore the catalogue** area by entering your search term and an optional range of dates. On the right-hand side of this screen is the link to research guides which can be very useful to family historians.

Find online collections

Go back to the website's home screen and click on **Find online** collections. The screen that is displayed has a list of topics on the left-hand side of the screen. On the right-hand side are more details of some of the online collections. However, not all are available on the National Archives' website and you may be referred to websites such as Findmypast or Ancestry. If there are documents within the National Archives online collection, you may have to pay for a download from the their website.

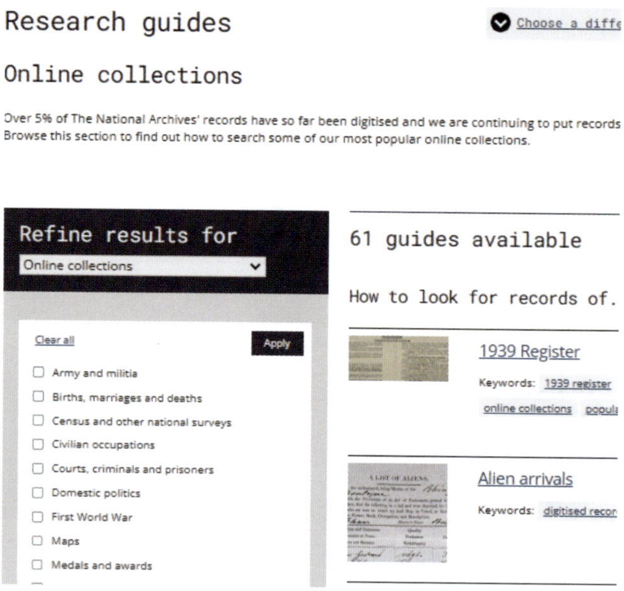

In the **Refine results for** column, click the boxes for **First World War** and **Medals and awards** as shown below. Then click the **Apply** button.

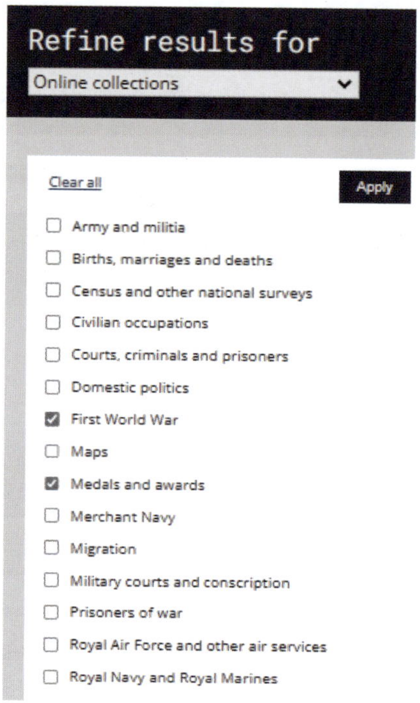

This is the screen which shows the available guides

3 guides available

How to look for records of...

British Army medal index cards 1914-1920

Keywords: digitised records   online collections   ✔ All records viewable online

British Army nurses' service records 1914-1918

Keywords: digitised records   online collections   ✔ All records viewable online

Household Cavalry soldiers' service records 1799-1920

Keywords: digitised records   online collections   ✔ All records viewable online

Military Records

The National Archives website provides some information on military records. On the home screen, click on **Search the Catalogue**. Part of the web page you will see is shown on the next page.

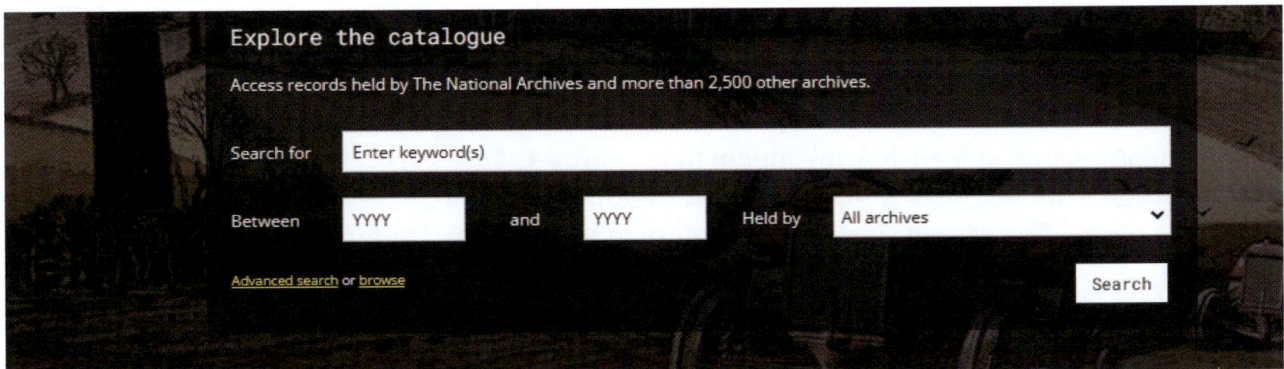

Explore the catalogue

Access records held by The National Archives and more than 2,500 other archives.

Search for   Enter keyword(s)

Between   YYYY   and   YYYY   Held by   All archives

Advanced search or browse   Search

Popular collections

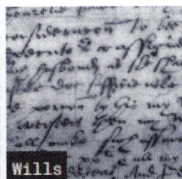

Medals   Wills

Royal Navy service records   RAF combat reports

What is Discovery?

Discovery holds more than 32 million descriptions of records held by The National Archives and more than 2,500 archives across the country. Over 9 million records are available for download.

Frequent searches

World War One army service records

Escape and evasion reports

Passenger lists

Merchant navy service

Research guides

Our guides are a great place to start your research. What are you looking for?

Family history

First World War

In the **Research guides** column, click the **First World War** picture and this screen will be displayed.

First World War

Learn how to find and understand records of soldiers and sailors, battles and battalions and almost every other aspect of the British perspective on the Great War.

Refine results for	56 guides available
First World War ⌄	How to look for records of... ☐ Show only guides with all records online
Clear all Apply	**Recommended guide** First World War – an overview Keywords: first world war wars world war one
☐ Army	British and Commonwealth prisoners of the First World War and previous wars
☐ Births, marriages and deaths	Keywords: first world war prisoners of war world war one
☐ Foreign and colonial affairs	British Army medal index cards 1914-1920
☐ Home front	Keywords: digitised records online collections ✔ All records viewable online
☐ Intelligence services	British Army nurses
☐ Maps, plans and land	Keywords: army british army nurses women's military service
☐ Medals and awards	British Army nurses' service records 1914-1918
☐ Merchant Navy	Keywords: digitised records online collections ✔ All records viewable online
☐ Military courts and conscription	
☐ Nursing	
☐ Prisoners of war and internees	
☐ Royal Air Force and other air services	
☐ Royal Navy and Royal Marines	
Clear all Apply	

The **First World War – an overview** is worth reading if you are new to the topic.

Neither of my grandfathers took part in the First World War and their children were too young. So I have picked another name, Frederick George WOOTTON, from my family tree to show you how to use the National Archives.

We are going to look at **British Army medal index cards 1914 – 1920.** Click this option to display information on the records. If you scroll down, you will find a place where you can enter your ancestor's name. This screen shows you my entry in the **Details of individual** box.

How do I search the records?

You can search for an individual medal index card using the form below. You do not need to fill out every field to search these records; using only the last name and regiment number often works. Your search results will be displayed in Discovery, our catalogue. From search results you can select an individual record (by clicking on the title) and download it (charges apply).

Details of individual:

First name	Frederick George
Last name	Wootton
Regimental number	
Corps	
Rank/unit	

Search

I was lucky with this individual as only one record is found as shown below.

Records 1 | Record creators 0

Descriptions of records and information about how to access them

1 - 1 of 1 results Sorted by: Relevance Simple view Print Export results

Medal card of Wootton, Frederick George. Corps: Royal Warwickshire Regiment attached Oxfordshire and Buckinghamshire Light...

War Office: Service Medal and Award Rolls Index, First World War. Wilson F - Zzdey S. Medal card of Wootton, Frederick George. Corps Regiment No Rank Royal Warwickshire Regiment attached Oxfordshire and Buckinghamshire Light Infantry 42050 Private.

Document type: M

Held by:	The National Archives, Kew - War Office, Armed Forces, Judge Advocate General, and related bodies
Date:	1914 - 1920
Reference:	WO 372/22/73560
Subjects:	Armed Forces (General Administration) | Army | Conflict | Medals | Operations, battles and campaigns

Click on the title in blue to view the medal card. This will take you to a web page where you can download an image of the medal index card.

The medal card will give you information as to the regiment your ancestor served in and his regimental number; you can use this unique number to search other sites including Ancestry which has images of the attestation forms and other military records if available for the individual concerned.

Royal Navy Records

Go back to the website's home screen and click **Search the catalogue** option.

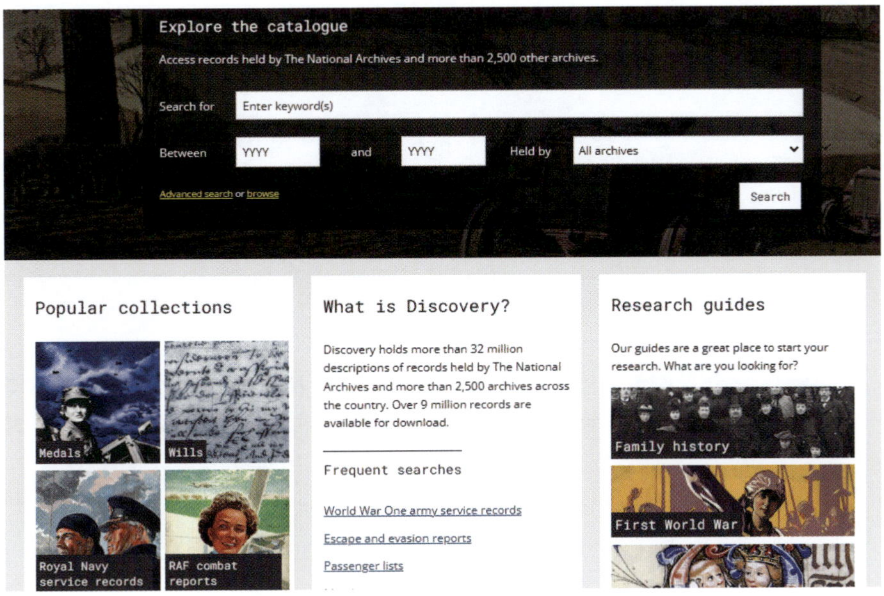

On the left-hand side of the screen you will see a picture with the title **Royal Navy service records**. Click on that and this is the screen you will see.

How to look for records of...

Contact us for advice

Royal Navy ratings' service records 1853-1928

How can I view the records covered in this guide?

✔ View Online   ✘ Order copies   ✔ Visit us in Kew   ✔ Pay for research

How many are online?   None   Some   **All**

Still need help?

Live chat
For quick pointers
Tuesday to Saturday
09:00 to 17:00

Live chat now

What are these records?

Available here are over 700,000 Royal Navy service records for ratings who **entered** the service between 1853 and 1928. Some of the records cover periods of service up to at least 1950.

The original records are in four series at The National Archives:

- continuous service engagement books from 1853 to 1872, in series ADM 139
- registers of seamen's services from 1873 to 1924, in series ADM 188
- registers of seamen's services from 1925-1928, in series ADM 362
- continuous record (CR) cards from 1929-1950, in series ADM 363

Please note, a rating must have **enlisted before 1929** in order to have a record within these series.

Email
For more detailed research enquiries.

@

Related research guides

Royal Navy ratings of the First World War

Royal Navy ratings up to 1913

Royal Navy ratings enlisted after 1918

Scroll down to find where you can enter your ancestor's name. I found that Louisa CREBER's father was in the navy, so I entered his details into the search box as shown below.

Details of individual:

First name	James
Last name	Creber
Service number	
Place of birth	Devonport

Date (YYYY):

From	1850
To	1901

Search

Below is the result of the search and several James Creber records were displayed. However, you will notice that the date of birth is given so if you know that, you should be able to find your ancestor's record.

Name Creber, James. Place of Birth: Devonport, Devon. Continuous Service Number: 20884B. Date of Volunteering:...

Admiralty: Royal Navy Continuous Service Engagement Books. CS NUMBERS. 20801B - 20900B. Name Creber, James. Place of Birth: Devonport, Devon. Continuous Service Number: 20884B. Date of Volunteering: 10 September 1872. Date of Birth: 02 August 1837.

Location: Devonport, Devon

Held by:	The National Archives, Kew - Admiralty, Navy, Royal Marines, and Coastguard
Date:	1853 - 1872
Reference:	ADM 139/1009/20884

Name Creber, James. Place of Birth: Devonport, Devon. Continuous Service Number: 25376. Date of Volunteering:...

Admiralty: Royal Navy Continuous Service Engagement Books. CS NUMBERS. 25301 - 25400. Name Creber, James. Place of Birth: Devonport, Devon. Continuous Service Number: 25376. Date of Volunteering: 13 November 1855. Date of Birth: 03 June 1839.

Location: Devonport, Devon

Held by:	The National Archives, Kew - Admiralty, Navy, Royal Marines, and Coastguard
Date:	1853 - 1872
Reference:	ADM 139/254/25376

In fact the second record is the one for my ancestor. Once again clicking on the blue title will take you to a screen where you can order a copy of the image. In my case it was a full history of his Royal Naval career.

What do I do now?

Take a deep breath and be pleased and proud of what you have achieved so far without spending much money. I have shown you the basic records that you can access freely and with minimal cost. However, to make further progress on your research, you will probably have to turn to commercial websites like Ancestry and others; this means you will have to pay to view some documents in detail.

I have listed the most useful websites you could use in the appendix. I have also recommended some books on the subject – but there are hundreds to choose from, so contemplate a visit to your local library too.

You should join your local family history society, and perhaps the society in the area in which your ancestors lived as well. For a modest annual subscription, these groups usually publish a regular magazine, allow access to additional members only information on their websites and other society publications pertinent to their area.

You could also subscribe to a commercial family history magazine and the most popular ones are listed in the appendix.

Finally, I have listed some useful websites on computer software family history programs.

Conclusion

Do you remember the first-ever bicycle you had as a child? Most people do...you probably remember seeing it for the first time in its new and bright colours. You can picture the exact place where eventually you rode it all by yourself - and what a thrill that was! Researching your ancestors is a bit like learning to ride a bike. It's new, it's exciting and you will definitely endure a few knocks, bumps and falls along the way until you reach your goal of finding a specific ancestor.

Tackling your family history is a vast project to undertake – and even more so for someone who is completely new to the subject. *How do I start? How do I actually do it? Where do I look? What will I find?* These are the sorts of questions beginners always ask – and I believe my book has the answers!

I have tried to explain simple ways to approach your research which in turn will bring some light and clarity to what at first seems an impossible problem. The chapters have been devised in a systematic way, taking you one step at a time, guiding you in the research process. The exercises at the end of each chapter are not difficult; they are designed to give you a bit of practice at using free websites before you tackle your own ancestors. And they are fun to do! The answers to the exercises are at the end of the book...no peeking first!!

You will also find various appendixes at the back of book including a list of useful websites, suggested further reading on the topic, and advice on what to do next and how to make further progress with your project.

I heard someone once say...*those dead people will always be out there, just waiting to be found!* So whatever you do – never give up!!

The rewards and benefits are definitely worth it...just like your first solo bike ride all those years ago! Happy researching and good luck!

Answers to Exercises

Exercise 2

The family tree should look like this. The numbers refer to the numbered paragraphs in the exercise. These show where and how the information in the conversation was revealed.

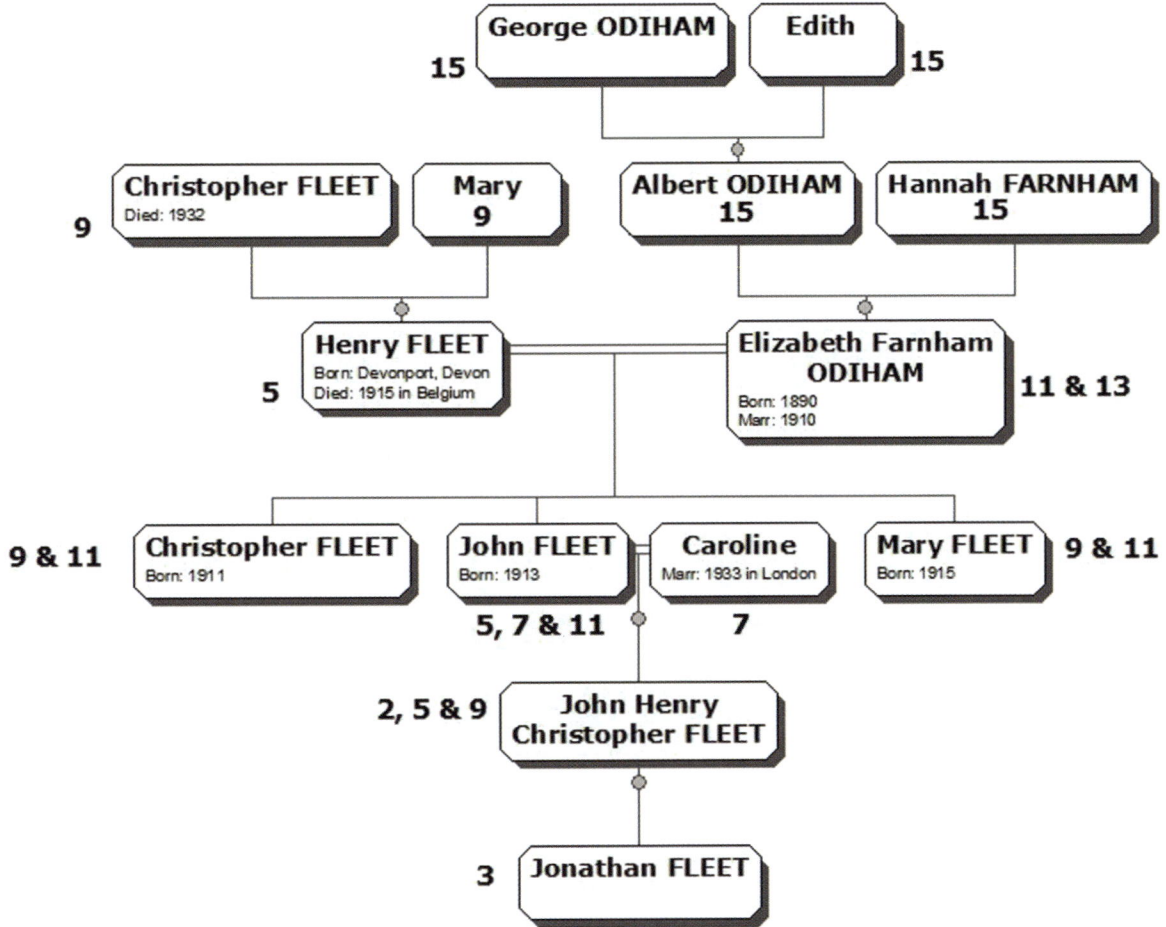

```
                              ┌─────────────────┐ ┌──────────┐
                           15 │ George ODIHAM   │ │  Edith   │ 15
                              └─────────────────┘ └──────────┘
                                        └───────────┬─────────┘
┌──────────────────┐ ┌──────────┐       ┌──────────────────┐ ┌────────────────────┐
│ Christopher FLEET│ │   Mary   │       │  Albert ODIHAM   │ │  Hannah FARNHAM     │
│ Died: 1932       │ │    9     │       │       15         │ │        15           │
└──────────────────┘ └──────────┘       └──────────────────┘ └────────────────────┘
 9        └──────────────┬──────────┘            └─────────────┬────────────┘
              ┌────────────────────────┐         ┌────────────────────────────┐
              │ Henry FLEET            │─────────│ Elizabeth Farnham          │
              │ Born: Devonport, Devon │         │       ODIHAM               │
         5    │ Died: 1915 in Belgium  │         │ Born: 1890                 │ 11 & 13
              └────────────────────────┘         │ Marr: 1910                 │
                                                 └────────────────────────────┘
        ┌──────────────────┬──────────────────┬──────────────────┐
┌──────────────────┐ ┌──────────────┐ ┌──────────────┐ ┌──────────────┐
│ Christopher FLEET│ │ John FLEET   │─│  Caroline    │ │ Mary FLEET   │  9 & 11
│ Born: 1911       │ │ Born: 1913   │ │ Marr: 1933   │ │ Born: 1915   │
└──────────────────┘ └──────────────┘ │ in London    │ └──────────────┘
 9 & 11                5, 7 & 11       └──────────────┘
                                        7
                     ┌──────────────────────┐
         2, 5 & 9    │ John Henry           │
                     │ Christopher FLEET    │
                     └──────────────────────┘
                              │
                     ┌──────────────────┐
                  3  │ Jonathan FLEET   │
                     └──────────────────┘
```

You were asked to identify what information was missing and what you would need to find out to verify and confirm the facts. The answers are on the next page.

Issue	Record needed
Is Mary John's twin or was she born in 1915?	Birth reference or certificate
Are George and Edith parents of Albert Odiham or Hannah Farnham?	Marriage certificate of Albert and Hannah to give you the names of their fathers
When was Elizabeth Farnham Odiham born?	Birth reference or certificate
When was Henry Fleet born?	Birth reference or certificate
When did Henry Fleet die?	Death reference or certificate
What is Caroline's maiden name?	Marriage reference or certificate
Who did Christopher Fleet marry?	Marriage reference or certificate
When did Elizabeth Farnham Odiham die?	Death reference or certificate

Exercise 3

1. Alfred Joseph **Hitchcock**   birth Dec 1899 W. Ham 4a 320

2. Thomas **Hardy**   birth Jun 1840 Dorchester 8 51

3. Sir Jesse **Boot**   birth Sep 1850 Nottingham 15 611

4. John James **Sainsbury**   birth Sep 1844 Lambeth 4 298

5. William Gilbert **Grace**   birth Sep 1848 Keynsham 11 128

6. Arthur Neville **Chamberlain** birth Jun 1869 King's N. 6c 407

    Neville Chamberlain's children
    - Dorothy E   birth Mar 1912 King's N. 6c 846
    - Francis M   birth Jun 1914 Kings N. 6d 153
    - *Francis N   birth Jun 1914 Kings N. 6d 153*

    NOTE: *There are two entries for the child Francis because the transcriber could not decide on the correct middle initial. Remember...only initials are given for the children's second names, so make sure you record what you see, not what you think should be there!*

7. Clement Richard **Attlee**   birth Mar 1883 Wandsworth 1d 785

    Clement Attlee's children
    - Janet H   birth Mar1923 W.Ham 4a 839
    - Felicity A   birth Sep 1925 W.Ham 4a 740
    - Martin R   birth Sep 1927 W.Ham 4a 628
    - Alison E   birth Jun 1930 W.Ham 4a 633

8. Margaret H **Roberts**   birth Dec 1925 Grantham 7a 673
    Muriel J Roberts   birth Jun 1921 Grantham 7a 904

If you had difficulty finding any of the above, try again now you know the answers.

Exercise 4

1. Arthur Neville **Chamberlain**
   Marriage Mar 1911 St.Geo.H.Sq. 1a 662 [Note year]
   Married **Annie** V Cole [Note his wife's correct first name.]
   Death Dec 1940 Aldershot 2c 599 aged 71

2. Karl **Marx**
   Death Mar 1883 Pancras 1b 136 aged 64

3. Clementine **Hozier** married Winston Leonard S Churchill.
   Sep 1908 St. Geo. H. Sq 1a 1110

4. Emmeline **Goulden** married Richard Marsden Pankhurst.
   Dec 1879 Salford 8d 154

5. Maria Elizabeth **Dickin** married Arnold Francis Dickin.
   Sep 1899 St Geo. H. Sq. 1a 1118
   Remember first cousins can have the same surname.

6. Charles **Babbage**
   Death Dec 1871 Marylebone 1a 383 aged 79

7. Margaret Thatcher's parents married Jun 1917 Grantham 7a 938.
   Alfred **Roberts** married Beatrice E Stephenson.

8. Clement **Attlee**
   Clement R *Attles* married Violet H Millar.
   Mar 1922 Hampstead 1a 1073.
   Note: *Incorrect spelling of Attlee's surname but shown correctly against his wife's entry.*
   Death Dec 1967 Westminster 5e 918 aged 84

Exercise 5

Family Search answers

1. Downe AKA Down, Kent, England

2. Queen's Cres, St Pancras, London, Middlesex (John J born 1845)

3. Trinity Road, Wandsworth, Surrey (born 1841)

4. Stapleton Rd, St Philip & Jacob (Out), Gloucestershire (Wm G so try W* G as the first name)

5. Chester Road, Stretford, Lancashire

6. St James's Place, Westminster, London, Middlesex (William Master Churchill aged 6)

Exercise 6

FreeCEN answers

1. Victoria Terrace, Godshill, I O W, Hampshire

    RG 09 600 Folio 41 Page 33

2. 6 Peel Street, St Peter, Bedford

    RG 12 1249 Folio 21 Page 25

3. Beatrice Road, Kempston, Bedford, Bedfordshire

    RG 12 1250 Folio 111 Page 6

Exercise 7

1. Name at baptism - Charles Robt. **Darwin**
    Date baptised 15 Nov 1809   Date born 12 Feb 1809
    Church/parish - Saint Chad, Shrewsbury, Shropshire, England
    Parents: Father Robt. Darwin. Mother Susannah

2. Name at baptism - Robert **Peel**
    Date baptised 28 Mar 1788   Date born 05 Feb 1788
    Church/parish - Saint Mary, Bury, Lancashire, England
    Parent: Father Robt. Peel

NOTE: *Be aware the correct record might not be at the top of the list and there could be more than one entry, as is the case for Robert Peel.*

3. Name at baptism - Isambard Kingdom **Brunel**
    Date baptised 01 Nov 1806   Date born 09 Apr 1806
    Church/parish - Saint Mary's, Portsea, Hampshire
    Parents: Father Marc Isambard Brunel. Mother Sophia

4. Name at baptism - Isaac **Newton**
    Date baptised   01 Jan 1642
    Church/parish - Colsterworth, Lincoln
    Parents: Father Isaac Newton. Mother Hanna

5. Name at baptism - Jane **Austen**
    Date baptised - 17 Dec 1775
    Church/parish - Steventon, Hampshire
    Parents: Father Geo Austen. Mother Cassa

Note: *Her father's name is given as Geo. This may well be short for George but always record what you actually see in your search results. The same principle applies to the father of Robert Peel where his father was noted as Robt. Peel.*

Suggested further reading and useful website links

Useful books for beginners

Christian, Peter and Annal, David. *Census – A Family Historian's Guide* Bloomsbury (2014)

Fowler, Simon. *Tracing Your Ancestors* Pen & Sword (2011)

Osborn, Helen. *Genealogy – Essential Research Methods* Hale (2012)

Paton, Chris. *Tracing Your Family History on the Internet* Pen & Sword (2022)

Probert, Rebecca. *Marriage Law for Genealogists* Takeaway.(2012)

Raymond, Stuart. *Introducing Family History* Family History Books (2020)

Scott, Jonathan. *The Family History Web Directory* Pen & Sword (2016)

Visit your library and see what they have before you contemplate purchasing any books.

Useful websites covering many aspects of family history

www.familyhistoryfederation.com/societies-az

Join a family history society where you live and the area where your ancestors lived. The Family History Federation's main website and link above give a list of all member societies

www.familyhistoryfederation.com/resources-research-online-resources

They can help with **free** resources too!

www.familyhistorybooksonline.com

Part of the Family History Federation. Worth a browse at their titles as they often have books on offer at cheaper prices!

Some towns may have a U3A group where you could meet fellow genealogists.

Many libraries provide **free** access to one or more library versions of the "big" commercial websites like Ancestry and Findmypast.

www.ancestry.co.uk/search/collections/

www.findmypast.co.uk/search/historical-records?

www.thegenealogist.co.uk

The Genealogist is another commercial website worth exploring.

www.familysearch.org/search/collection/list

Family Search is free to use and can be accessed at home.

www.parishchest.com

Part of the Family History Federation. Hosts many shops for family history societies and other suppliers.

https://genealogysupplies.com
This commercial supplier is particularly useful for computer software programs and other supplies you may wish to consider.

www.my-history.co.uk/
This company also specialises in genealogical supplies.

www.rootschat.com
This is a **free** website and covers a vast range of topics, places and all sorts of genealogical issues. If you are only just beginning your research, you probably won't need this site yet, but in an idle moment, have a look at it, click on the area or topic and see where it takes you!

Family History Magazines

Television programmes on family history have increased people's awareness of the hobby so many companies now publish monthly or bi-monthly magazines on the subject. They are full of useful information. Some of the main magazines are listed below:

Family Tree magazine (UK)
Who Do You Think You Are?
Discover Your Ancestors (periodical)

Computer Software for Family History

Recording your family history research results on computer software will eventually eliminate the need for all those notes and bits of paper you have accumulated. It's a good idea to look carefully at what each can provide and compare what they offer. Talk to other genealogists too and ask what they use and why. The main software programs are listed below – but there are others. Some will provide a free taster which allows you to enter a limited number of records to see if you like the program.

My Family Tree
Legacy 9
Rootsmagic
Family Tree Maker (UK edition)
Family Historian 7
Gramps
Mac Family Tree

Bibliography and sources

Ancestry	www.ancestry.co.uk/search
Cyndi's List	www.cyndislist.com
Family Search WiKi	www.familysearch.org/en/wiki/Main_Page
Family Search	www.familysearch.org.uk
Family History Federation	www.familyhistoryfederation.com
FindMyPast	www.findmypast.co.uk/search/
Free BMD	www.freebmd.org.uk
FreeCen	www.freecen.org.uk
FreeReg	www.freereg.org.uk
General Register Office	www.gro.gov.uk/gro/content
Genuki	www.genuki.org.uk
The National Archives	www.nationalarchives.gov.uk
UKBMD (local register office indexes)	www.UKBMD.org.uk/local_bmd
Wikipedia	www.wikipedia.org/wiki/genealogy

Illustration

The photograph of George and Louisa Trice at Marazion is the personal property of the author.

Publisher's Notes:

Image quality is not always sharp. Some screenshots from websites reproduce poorly in print. This is beyond our control and we apologise.

The website images used in this publication are for educational purposes. All are subject to copyright conditions which can be found on the respective websites.

Cyndi's List: www.cyndislist.com

Family Search: www.familysearch.org/legal/terms

FreeBMD, FreeREG and FreeCEN are all part of
www.freeukgenealogy.org where you will find their conditions.

General Register Office:
www.gro.gov.uk/gro/content/certificates/copyright.asp

GenUKI: www.genuki.org.uk/org/help/reference/copyrightnotice

The National Archives: www.nationalarchives.gov.uk/legal/

NOTES

NOTES

NOTES

NOTES

NOTES